MEDIA FLOW AND MONITORING

MEDIA FLOW AND MONITORING

ARUN BHATIA

AKANSHA PUBLISHING HOUSE
NEW DELHI

AKANSHA PUBLISHING HOUSE
R 37-B, Vani Vihar, Uttam Nagar
New Delhi-110059
Email: ektabooks@yahoo.com

Showroom
4649/21B, Ansari Road
Darya Ganj
New Delhi - 110 002
Ph.: 23269193 / 9811582579

Media Flow and Monitoring

First Edition 2005
ISBN 81-8370-022-5

[he responsibility for the facts stated, conclusions reached etc. is entirely that of the Author. The publisher is not responsible for them, whatsoever.]

PRINTED IN INDIA

Published by M.P. Misra for Akansha Publishing House, New Delhi and
Printed at **: Mehra Offset Press, New Delhi.**

Contents

Preface

The broad look at the book on international flow of media materials and the rest focusing on to the emerging areas of media, and monitoring of media performance. The time have indeed bypassed the mechanistic flow studies which were fashionable until the 1980s and that the process of audiovisual communication in the contemporary world is quite complicated and full of paradoxes. At the same time the book can be taken as reminders of the long passage to be made from past research tradition to presenting a coherent and convincing alternative.

International journalism has recently shown inadequacy in connection with major conflicts of the world. The public relations agencies have appeared as a new element in news manipulation. That is why the monitoring of the media has become more crucial to keep the action of the media in proper way. This book presents and clarifies some dimensions that should be taken into account in any effort to establish a system of media monitoring. To monitor is to understand in order to act in an informed, well reasoned way. The book is having extensive issues with exceptionally international character.

Editor

1

Media Monitoring

The criteria of the surrounding inter-human society, and not only of the clients, will always play a role. A profession will never be permitted to be self-contained, being accountable only to itself. Actually, neither will nations: surrounding inter- nation society also imposes standards and demands accountability. And there will be paradigm shifts within the profession, pitting younger generations with new standards against the interests of the older generation.In short: watchful eyes everywhere.

International journalism has recently shown its inadequacy in connection with two major conflicts in a way which should have led to major revolts and agonizing reappraisals. In the Second Gulf War, 17 January to 27 February 1991, the problem was not the infamous Pentagon pooling system, based on journalists they could trust, thereby engineering the outcome.

To blame a machine made for war "with all necessary means" for including manipulation of the news process among those means is like blaming a lion for not being vegetarian. The problem is the high level of acceptance among journalists, the low number who tried to obtain, often at considerable risk, independent access to the events. And that acceptance seems to have run through the whole news chain, via agencies and editors to the end users.

No massive refusal among journalists to use the pool system, no massive rejection of the highly orchestrated news conferences, no massive protests among readers/viewers/listeners have been reported. And this in presumably free societies! In countries occupied by Nazi-Germany during the Second World War there was at least massive skepticism of the official media, and in addition an alternative, illegal press assembled and distributed at even higher risks.

Whereas this was a clear case of the State manipulating what will reach Civil Society via the Media, the Yugoslav War offers another, equally or more discomforting picture of how Capital can manipulate. The classic techniques are obvious: buying space for publicity; buying space for an article; buying a journalist; buying an editor; buying a paper; a radio or TV station; buying a whole news chain; buying a cartel of news chains.

But this time something else has entered the news chain: public relations agencies, with States as clients, constructing a virtual reality by systematically planting non-events as news, or changing focus and discourse in favor of their clients.

Monitoring goes beyond merely recording. To monitor is to characterize something according to a criterion. In other words, monitoring means evaluating. We are doing it all the time: mapping others, individuals or collectivities, media, sometimes ourselves, mapping events like meals, contexts like restaurants on dichotomies of good-bad or on more refined scales of judgment. And of course, evaluation is judgmental. Equally obviously, the criteria chosen for the evaluation, the value-dimensions, are subjective, coming out of the attitudes/assumptions of some individual or collectivity. But given the value-dimensions, the mapping may be consensual.

If we should monitor monitoring, would the term "objective" be useful? Maybe as a term, but then that term has to be understood properly; anchoring "objective" in what is intersubjectively communicable and reproducible. This means: (1) the value-dimensions used for evaluation must be explicit; (2) the mapping process on the value-dimensions must be explicit.

Only by making the whole process explicit, openly formulated and accessible, is communication among subjects possible, and only under that condition can other subjects, using the same definitions and the same procedures arrive at the same results, i.e., mappings on the value-dimensions, evaluations, monitoring. Are they the media researchers supposedly doing the job of monitoring? They would definitely be among the subjects communicating criteria and mapping media, presumably being competent to do so. But the whole process is too important to be limited to researchers as the competence group.

In other words, not only researchers who have the news chain as their subject area but the subjects along the news chain, event-makers, news-makers and news-consumers should understand and preferably agree that the dimensions are not only meaningful but important. Of course, that does not mean that there will be consensus about the dimensions. The goal is not consensus but a fruitful dialogue among everybody concerned, adding and subtracting dimensions:

A good example is the monitoring of "development" of countries. There is no consensus that "GNP/capita" is the only or the basic value-dimension. But by making this dimension explicit economists have done a great service to the debate: those who have read and understood the definition to the point of being able to carry out the operations agree atleast on what they are talking about.

Out of this fifty years old debate has grown a vast range of additional value-dimensions, many of them reflected in the very interesting Human Development Report issued annually by the United Nations Development

Program. But having said that the other side of the coin should also be mentioned: a dialogue focussed on development indicators may become philosophically flat, losing the deeper aspects of what is being discussed. Listing many aspects of "developed countries", "good media" can never fully substitute for a definition in intension, trying to get at the deeper meaning.

Monitoring Media

Imagine somewhere in the world there is a very big matrix recording the evaluation of media on n value-dimensions; both m and n being very high. The media may operate with hourly, daily, weekly, monthly, annual or other frequencies, so each cell in the matrix accmmodates evaluation on one value-dimension over time.

In each cell therewould be a curve with time on the horizontal and the value-dimension onthe vertical axis. In principle there could be any possible curve shape: an optimistic upwards tilt, a downward trend, "the best/worst is behind us", no trend at all. A comparison can be made with charts for economic growth, trade balance, unemployment, or any economic indicator, or with human rights monitoring of all countries on all articles in the human rights declaration/conventions. Some criteria are easily agreed on:

— all three media, papers/TV/radio should be monitored

— those with the largest circulation/audience should be included

— those usually considered elite/high quality should be included

— media seen as competitors should be included, also to stimulate interest in the monitoring process

— different areas of the world should be included

— from each area representative local media should be included

Even to monitor one medium, like "the world's news leader" might be interesting. Add to that another TV station from a different civilization for contrast, and the process of monitoring becomes more than just a set of data. To be fair to the media and to the users, the definition of media should be kept open.

Most studies are done of newspapers at the expense of magazines and journals, of newscasts less than of commentary, and the major source of information for most people, other people, in formal meetings as well as informal gossip, are usually left out. This is in line with the focus on literacy rather than orality and on visuality rather than literacy. But studies should also be made to give people a voice as to their sources of information.

Of course, these are very general dimensions. Particular issues would call for more specificity. But even so this more general form of monitoring might be useful. Some retroactive monitoring back to earlier decades, even centuries, might also be interesting. Could there be an increasing tendency toward more concentrated ownership and sources of income, toward more advertising and less interaction with the users, toward more partisan media, more sensationalism in general?

Less focus on possible solutions, more on problems; less on resolutions, more on conflicts? We shall never know the extent of influence from outside the media. But we can know something about the result, the face showing to the public, the entry into public space.

Thus, monitoring should be done in such a way that it is comparative, and not only across media space today, but through time, diachronically as well as synchronically. Only in this way can certain tendencies be uncovered that would make monitoring not only useful but absolutely crucial. We may argue over how good or bad is the present situation, but agree on the need to do something should the tendencies continue in the same direction. And the same applies to space: if the patterns differ from one civilization to the next, even among countries in the same civilization, then monitoring may be an invitation not so much to social control as to social learning.

The purpose of this chapter has only been to clarify some of the dimensions that would have to be taken into account in any effort to establish a system of media monitoring. It is written in an actor-oriented style: editors and journalists act, people monitor to register media behavior. Writing this way by no means implies a general actor orientation in analyzing media in particular and communication in general.

Actors are free to act, but only up to a certain point. The rest is determined by structure and culture, and other factors. Not only event-makers, news-producers, and news-consumers are influenced by deep structure and deep culture, by conflicting interests, profit motives, poor vs rich discources in the general culture, etc. So is the monitor; so is the author of these lines. Nobody is totally free, above such factors.

But the idea behind monitoring is not to theorize, but to provide data that may serve as raw material for such theories. More particularly, with rich material the analyst can use a very powerful method: differential analysis: why is Media A different from Media B, in countries C and D, but not in E and F; and why does that difference seem to increase over time?

The richer the statistical material, the deeper the findings that can be extracted; and above some dimensions about the media rather than the items appearing have been indicated. Monitoring is much more than trend-watching: to monitor is to understand in order to act in an informed, well reasoned way. Monitoring is beyond mirroring what happens in the fourth pillar of society. To monitor the media is to make them transparent: a basic condition for democracy to function.

2

Media Performance

Media Monitoring Project (MMP)

The Media Monitoring Project (MMP) was the leading organisation monitoring the total output of news in radio, television and print before and during South Africa's first democratic elections in April 1994. The main objective of the MMP was to monitor the vertical top-down distribution of information from powerful media institutions to citizens many of whom were first-time voters, the majority illiterate, unfamiliar with the concept of human rights and not accustomed to the language of democracy.

After the elections the MMP has had to change its role from vertical to horizontal monitoring and to observe the equal distribution of information to all citizens, and from all citizens, and ensure that channels of access are available to all citizens. From the time that the National Party government assumed power in 1948 the broadcast media have been perceived to be the voice of the state. When television was finally introduced in 1976, state skills in utilising the broadcast media for propaganda purposes had become finely tuned. However, little consistent monitoring of radio and television was undertaken although several newspapers expressed concern about the disproportionate time devoted to editorialising, as against hard news, in South Africa Broadcasting (SABC) broadcasts. The Star newspaper as early as 1976 found that South African cabinet ministers were getting nearly 10 times more exposure on television than spokespersons for all the country's opposition parties combined. The calculations found that: In 24 newscasts cabinet ministers were featured 38 times for a total of 27 minutes. Compared with this, United Party spokespersons were featured 6 times, for a total time of about 2 minutes. Some of the strategies used by SABC:

— The promotion of government viewpoints by quoting its ministers and officials while generally not recording or inviting the views of its critics.

— The promotion of pro-government black spokespersons while ignoring black government critics.

— Using material that discredited foreign governments that were critical of apartheid.

— Giving prominence to violence, social discord, race problems and oppression elsewhere, while playing down similar problems related to the Nationalist government's policies.

— Promoting the spectre of Communism.

— Black-ruled countries in a way likely to create the impression that black rule is synonymous with violence, chaos and impoverishment.

The issue of state interference in news broadcasts was kept alive in the press during 1976. In 1977, with the prospect of an election to be held later in the year, Donald Woods, writing in The Daily Dispatch, stated:

> If you keep your eye on the television set you will find that the spokesmen of the pro-Nationalist 53 per cent of the white voters get something like 3000 per cent more opportunity to express their political views on TV than the spokesmen of the anti-Nationalist 47 per cent.

In 1977 a weekly television column, "On the Box with John van Zyl" started in The Star newspaper which was to consistently and critically analyze the output of SATV for fourteen years until 1991. In the face of the then upcoming election Rhodes University Journalism Department undertook a quantitative monitoring project in November 1977 under Professor Les Switzer. Although Jan Schutte, Deputy Director Programmes, repudiated the statement, the suspicion lingered that the SABC slavishly followed party lines.

If television is a prime source of information about candidates in a political campaign, one might well question how effectively SABC television is fulfilling this function in terms of the 1977 election in South Africa? In 1989 the Institute for A Democratic Alternative in South Africa (IDASA) commissioned the Media Studies unit of the School of Dramatic Art of the University of the Witwatersrand to monitor the general elections. The resulting document showed quite conclusively the nature and extent of the blatant support given to the Nationalist Party by SABC-TV. Sophisticated propaganda strategies were employed by SABC-TV news managers, backed by similar radio programmes.

BMP

Two years later, in 1991, partly as a result of the IDASA project, a concerted monitoring project, initiated and funded by Hylton Appelbaum of the Liberty Life Foundation, was started at the Media Studies unit of the University of the Witwatersrand. The intention was basically a "watchdog" one which would look for bias and propaganda in television news and current affairs programmes specifically.

This reflected a perception that in spite of the unbanning of the ANC and other parties and the release of Nelson Mandela the previous year, the news department of the

SABC was still staffed by the same total onslaught warriors and the news did not represent the realities of the new South Africa. For instance, resistance in the so-called homelands to corruption and repression was seldom.

Monitoring Project (BMP) and it began to issue statements regularly to the media about examples of biased reporting. It opted for a combined qualitative and quantitative mode of analysis and adopted as a model the methodology devised for monitoring the 1989 elections for IDASA.

In January 1992 the BMP was represented at the Campaign for Open Media's (COM) "Free, Fair and Open Conference" and as a result monitored the SABC coverage of the whites-only referendum. In the hectic broadcasting negotiations that followed in 1993 between COM and others that resulted, for example, in the establishment of the Campaign for Independent Broadcasting and the appointment of a panel of eminent persons to select the new SABC Board, the European Community added considerable funding to the monitoring project through the COM.

This additional funding enabled the BMP to extend its monitoring activities. Although it had worked closely with the COM/CIB alliance and shared its democratic principles, it was decided that the BMP should be constituted independently and not aligned with any political party. On April 21st the BMP became an autonomous body. It then began to train a team of monitors and established regional teams in Natal and the Eastern Cape. Monitoring was extended beyond the main "white" English/Afrikaans television news on TV1 to the shorter news bulletins on the "black" CCV channel. This was soon extended to the four main black radio channels and ultimately to all of the radio channels and the main newspapers.

The original mission statement of the BMP arose from the need to assess the extent to which the SABC was fulfilling its obligations as a public broadcaster in terms of internationally accepted standards of promoting fairness, impartiality and diversity of opinions. The BMP believed that the SABC should be informed by the ideals of a non-racial, non-sexist, democratic South Africa which were fundamental to the reconstruction of the society. It acknowledged the United Nations Universal Declaration of Human Rights, particularly Article 19: Everyone has the right to freedom of opinion and expression, this right includes the right to hold opinions without interference and to seek, receive and impart information and ideas through any media and regardless of frontiers.

This, together with other Human Rights conventions like the 1978 UNESCO "Declaration on Fundamental Principles concerning the Contribution of the Mass Media..." in its entirety were taken as forming the mission statement of the BMP.In an internal document approved by the Board of Trustees at that time the BMP stated that it was essential that first-time voters be informed about issues of national importance and that it had set itself the task of analyzing news coverage and publicising the results in order to enhance public awareness about the manner in which the media were the political situation. It stressed that it was particularly concerned with monitoring the news and current affairs output of the publicly funded SABC radio and TV stations in view of its history of propaganda and being the mouthpiece of the Nationalist party.

The SABC with 8.8 million television viewers and 12.3 million daily radio listeners had a monopoly over the airwaves. In addition, since most South Africans were functionally illiterate and large sections of rural South Africa had limited access to newspapers, SABC radio news was often the sole source of information. Recognising that the SABC existed in a particular context and time in South African history, the MMP noted Resolution 4.301 adopted in 1970 by the General Conference of UNESCO which states that the mass media can make a fundamental contribution to the furthering of international understanding and cooperation in the interests of peace and human welfare.

Since the SABC had played an active role in disseminating information which helped maintain the apartheid system it has an added obligation to redress past information imbalances. As Article 2 of the UNESCO Paris Declaration of 1978 states:

> The mass media throughout the world, by reasons of their role, contribute to promoting human rights, in particular by giving expression to oppressed peoples who struggle against colonialism, neo-colonialism, foreign occupation and all forms of racial discrimination and oppression and who are unable to make their voices heard within their own territories.

Furthermore, the BMP believed that the SABC, as public service broadcasting was obliged to represent the colonial and political aspirations of the whole population. It had the obligation to "level the information playing field" by redressing racial cultural and political myths propagated during the apartheid regime. Lastly, the SABC had historically been the propaganda arm of the Nationalist Party government. This had resulted in an imbedded "naturalised" news culture, so pervasive as to be invisible to the journalists involved it. This meant that even sincere attempts to reform news from within would probably take some time to be effective. The BMP therefore had both an educative as well as monitoring role with regard to the SABC.

Categories of News Stories

There are three categories of news stories as the focus of its analysis. During 1992 and 1993, political violence in South Africa soared. The violence involved political organisations as well as state structures and therefore had a profound impact on the progress of the constitutional negotiations process. The first category which the project focused on was news coverage of violence. This included an assessment of the presentation of the various players, the extent of the coverage given to violent incidents, the context provided to the causes of the violence and the manner in which perpetrators and victims of violence were portrayed on SABC.

The second category was an assessment of the representation of the political scenario in the country-particularly, the portrayal of the transition process. The coverage of the minority parliament, government and structures of apartheid such as the homelands and self-governing territories was also examined. This area of analysis laid the groundwork for the project's focus on the coverage of the election.

The third category was an analysis of how the SABC was responding to the changing socio-economic environment in the country. SABC coverage of various socio-economic issues, such as housing, social services, poverty, and labour was assessed in terms of the priority afforded to them by the SABC and the discourse through which the issues were represented.

The BMP was always concerned that its research not just be an academic exercise but that it be distributed to those organisations with an interest in the transformation of the South African media. To this end, every two weeks to a wide variety of political, media, academic and monitoring organisations, as well as the SABC's board and editorial management. A bi-monthly newsletter reviewing particular aspects of news coverage and commenting on the process of change within the SABC was also sent out.

At the end of 1993, the then BMP released a news entitled "6 Months of the New SABC". SABC news and current affairs coverage in the six months since the new board of control had assumed office. The found that there had been "little substantial change in either radio or television news broadcasts", that "many of the old-style myths and prejudices were still evident in the news bulletins" and that "a bias towards the government is clearly manifest in much political reporting." The report stated that the SABC's institutional structure was one of the determining factors in its failure to reorient the content of its news programming.

The structural separations between broadcast channels at the SABC were one of the major problems influencing news coverage. On television there were clear racial and ethnic differences between CCV and TV1 (the "white" broadcasting service). The news bulletins were produced separately by black and white journalists and editorial teams which, aside from resulting in an unnecessary duplication of resources, often resulted in the development of "black news" and "white news".

There was a marked difference in coverage between the two news services. Black political parties received less time on TVl than on CCV, and traditionally white political parties were prioritised on TVl news. Moreover, the project provided several examples of cases in which TV1 and CCV had given differing, sometimes conflicting, perspectives on news issues of national importance.

Broadcast Monitoring Project over the past year has shown that SABC news services have revealed a distinct sympathy towards government and state institutions, while largely misrepresenting or under-representing opposition political organisations, particularly those organisations who have opposed apartheid in the past.

Simultaneously SABC has continued to perpetuate a racial division in its news coverage both by retaining an infrastructure that was essentially based on the policy of separate development, and by marginalising black society and perpetuating racist myths in its news coverage. Less than another six months later however, the MMP was to conclude that there had been an improvement in SABC news coverage and that the SABC and other media coverage of the election had been adequate.

Careful scrutiny and penetrating analysis of political claims and counter-claims were frequently lacking during the campaign. The role of the news media should be to provide information and analysis on the parties' policies. To do so, reporters must sift through a mountain of policies, statements, interviews, claim and counter claim-cut through the speculation, hype and rhetoric-to get to the real issues of the campaign.

But too often, political speeches or statements were reported without the real story being told. This lack of critical analysis meant the message was omitted. The presentation of policy took second place to a concentration on personalities or tangential issues. News became "event-driven" rather than "issue-driven."

The dominant issues for the media were those dealing with the political and electoral process itself. Only 38% of stories on television were deemed to have a clear reference to policy and over 60% of these involved issues to do with the political process. Relegated to virtual invisibility during the campaign were economic policy questions.

Politicians appeared frequently in the news and were too often allowed to set and control the news agenda. There was also lack of editorial initiative in evaluating, or relating the claims of politicians from different parties to each other, at least in the same story. Many stories had a simple source structure in which the political figures were able to put their views, without any counter-arguments, even by those they were making claims about.

Editorial Directions

Some South African media have a legacy of passive, obedient and unquestioning editorial practice. This manifested itself in a number of different ways: in the presentation of news and current affairs, in the quality of interviews, and in particular, the failure of the SABC to keep up with international stories, and in the broadcasters' ability to cover stories as they break.

News programmes were often slow off the mark to cover major events. On occasion, important stories were allowed to die because of an inability on the part of journalists to do follow-up legwork. Consequently, issues sometimes remained unresolved, statements unchallenged and the real story untold. In the electronic media, the major grist for the news-mill was provided by public occasions and the publicity seeking activities of political groups and institutions.

Three major categories could be distinguished. The first, comprising almost half of the news occasions reported, involved deliberate publicity moves and public campaigning. The second large group of news-generating occasions were formal meetings and the proceedings of political institutions, totalling about 20%. The third group of story occasions involved what can be broadly labelled as disorder news. Incidents of group violence (4%), strikes (5%) and other protest activity (5%) were the staples of this coverage.

The extent to which the electronic media were reacting blindly to media events constructed by major political players, and to obvious public events, was shown by the rarity of based primarily on media enterprise and in-depth journalism. Only two television stories were labelled as special media reports. None were specifically called special investigations.

The MMP was concerned that the reporting of some issues was so fragmented that it concealed or distorted the real story. This was especially true of the treatment of violence in Kwazulu/Natal by some media. The story was not an easy one to report on because of the remoteness of the area. The confused and uncertain situation was not helped by the contradictory statements of some party officials.

However, the fragmented way in which some of the South African media covered the incidents of violence and the comments of public figures did nothing to build a coherent picture of what was happening in the province. As part of its Interim Report, the MMP proposed four points as a media guide for reporting of violence. They were:

1. All victims of violence should be treated with equal dignity, irrespective of class, race and gender.
2. Forecasts and fears of violence must be treated with great caution by the media.
3. Media reporting should never treat the occurrence of violence with indifference, or imply an acceptance of its inevitability or acceptability.
4. As far as possible, media reporting should aim to make the incidents explicable to their audiences, to portray them with precision, and where necessary, pinpoint responsibility.

Sadly though, by the end of the election, there was very little improvement in violence reporting. Perhaps the most important problem that the SABC, and to a lesser extent the press, failed to counter, was the traditional apartheid separation of news audiences based on race.

Although newspapers, radio stations and television channels claimed their target audiences were not racially defined, the selection of news stories often betrayed a crude racial classification of their audience and did little to promote a common cause of democracy. Vast differences in line-ups, angle and tone were noticed frequently.

On the surface, the idea of a range of newsrooms exhibiting different approaches, values and attitudes has merit because of the diversity and choice it offers. However, if all it means is that each language group is provided with a single news focus based on a news editor's racially-based news judgement, there is no diversity, only biased reporting.

The MMP has associated itself with the world-wide move to ensure the quality of the provision of information and culture to all citizens. The Penang-based Third World Network is putting civil society interests on the agenda, and The People's Communication Charter initiative which was launched at the 1994 IAMCR Conference in Seoul can provide the basis for this sort of monitoring. The sort of horizontal monitoring that The People's Charter implies can be detected in its objectives:

— The Charter intended to contribute to a critical understanding of the significance of communication in the daily lives of individuals and peoples;
— The Charter articulates a shared position on communication from the perspective of people's interests and needs;
— The Charter aims to bring to (national and international) policy making processes a set of claims that represent people's fundamental right to communicate.

The MMP sees a clear purpose for itself in lobbying the media to guard the interests of the SA public, and monitoring whether they report events in South Africa in a fair and balanced fashion, informing citizens fully and properly. While the MMP cannot claim responsibility for the changes that have already taken place in the South African media, the project believes it played an important role in raising debates and interest in media issues. It will continue to do this.

3

Electronic Discussion Groups

The twentieth century, the growth in popularity of computer networking has been widely recognized. In developing countries, forty percent of households now own personal computers, while at least fifteen percent subscribe to an online service. The number of Internet users worldwide has expanded to more than thirty million and shows no sign of leveling off until well into the twenty-first century. In the past few years, telephone companies have had to meet shortages in the number of available telephone lines for modems by rapidly activating new area codes.

Further, some points out that international Internet growth is occurring at almost twice the rate of that in the U.S. Simultaneously, by most accounts, corporate intranet growth has skyrocketed: a survey in 1997 found that at least fifty percent of corporations planned to install company-wide networks by the end of that year. In 1999, these businesses are now rushing to place corporate web sites online so that they can "cash in" on the newly emerging global digital marketplace.

In the midst of these activities, a steady chorus of voices has continued to argue that digital networks should be employed to build communities characterized by free and equal participation. However, despite rhetoric promoting the emancipatory potential of digital networks, a survey of current computer-mediated communication (CMC) and group decision support system (GDSS) suggests that many theorists perpetuate transmissional/linear-flow or ritual/cultural conceptualizations of communication that may hinder theorizing about the process of online communication leading to community-building.

Electronic Discussion Groups (EDGs) and Online Communities

Computer-mediated communication (CMC) — broadly defined as the use of networked computers, in synchronous or asynchronous fashion, to send and receive text, audio, and/or video messages — was originally developed in the late 1960s. Early software packages utilized text interfaces that allowed users to type and send interactive messages, usually at quite slow baud rates; newer systems added videoconferencing and whiteboarding capabilities.

The most popular forms of computer mediated communication (CMC) to emerge were e-mail, newsgroups, and synchronous chat. Early systems included Turoff's Emergency Management Information System and Reference Index [EMISARI], EIES, and Engelbart's NLineSystem [NLS]). By the late 1970s/early 1980s, other systems emerged, including PLANET/FORUM, CONFER, ORACLE, CONCLAVE, BITNet, and a plethora of commercial offerings: the Source (later CompuServe), GEnie, the Whole Earth 'Lectric Link (WELL), and America OnLine (AOL) . Perhaps the most popular was the Usenet newsgroup system — developed in 1977 by programmers at Duke University and the University of North Carolina — which enabled users to read and post messages in an "electronic bulletin board".

By the late 1980s and early 1990s, grass roots political organizations began to form discussion forums, spearheaded in part by the National Public

Telecommunication Network (NPTN). These systems included the Santa Monica PEN (public electronic network), the Cleveland and Columbus FreeNets, the Seattle Community Network, and the Blacksburg, Virginia Electronic Network (BEN). Prominent international forums included GreenNet, NordNet, GlasNet, ComLink, GhastiNet, EcoNet, PeaceNet, ConflictNet, LaborNet, and WomenNet, among others.

The notion that electronic discussion groups, EDGs, fostered online — or virtual — communities circulated early in the development of computer networking. According to a philosophers and social scientists have long used the term community to characterize social interactions. He notes that scholars traditionally have advanced at least five different meanings for the term: a) the common people, b) a society or state, c) the members of a specific district, d) the "quality of holding something in common," and e) the "common identity and characteristics" of a group. Further, many scholars agree that nineteenth century German sociologist classic distinction between gemeinschaft/community and gesellschaft/society has had an important impact on current uses of the term.

One common finding is that computer-mediated communication (CMC) users experience a gemeinshaft-like "sense of community" through their online participation. Some argues that user appropriation of computer mediated communication (CMC) resources results in "emergent communities."

Dervin and Clark suggest an initial focus on micro-level communicative practices since social structures only exist via the engine of human action: A social structure that is not reenergized with acts of communicating dies; it simply does not exist. Structures are maintained, reified, rigidified, and changed through acts of communicating.

While acknowledging the importance of communication practice in the creation of online communities, many researchers borrow from theory that emphasizes what Dervin and Clark call the "nouns of communication" rather than the "verbs of communicating." The tendency among scholars is to see computer mediated communication (CMC) as either a process of message transmission or a site for emerging social/cultural formations. The problem with many computer mediated communication (CMC) studies is that they — quoting Carey — emphasize communication as "message transmission" rather than "'ritual . . . the sacred ceremony that draws persons together in fellowship and commonality'".

However, Dervin and Clark argue that both the "transmission" and "cultural" streams of communication studies "end up communication without communicating . . .": both have ignored the daily struggling step-takings — sometimes arduous, sometimes routinized, but never entirely unproblematic — by which individuals make sense of and live in their worlds and by which structures, cultures, and institutions are introduced, maintained and changed.

Transmission or ritual/cultural theories lead to findings that online communities emerge out of user a) exchange of factual and socio-emotional content via digital channels or b) adoption of online roles, rules, or identities. At best, both conclusions emphasize communicative states rather than processes. Both approaches emphasize the nouns of communication—messages, information, identities, social formations, netiquette, moderator roles, etc. — rather than the verbs of communicating — attending, creating ideas, expressing, finding connectedness, recalling, mediating, etc.

Dervin and Clark note that this tendency has operated as the primary Western communication model since the Enlightenment: "the founding fathers specified the structures they considered essential for democracy . . . . few of these specifications pertained to communication per se. Their world view found no necessity because for them in an open marketplace of ideas, correct ideas would by some magical process win".

Communication as human process usually gets short shrift. A closer look demonstrates the pervasiveness of the communication-as-noun perspective in computer mediated communication (CMC). Online contributions are often characterized as "messages" in "store and forward" information systems that are organized according to their "topic lines" or the date/time that a message was created. Online communities are assumed to be denoted by "threads" — the "main message"/"response" chains that coalesce around a specific topic, often measured by the number of "hits" a chain has accumulated.

Further, two of the most popular metaphors applied to electronic discussion groups (EDGs) — the "electronic bulletin board" and the "global public sphere" — both emphasize a noun-view of communication. The "bulletin board" metaphor reinforces the view that postings are "things" hung up on a virtual corkboard; the "global public sphere" metaphor emphasizes the space or locale where exchanges occur.

The problem caused by the pervasiveness of the noun-perspective in computer mediated communication (CMC) design was acknowledged by Hiltz and Turoff in a revealing passage: "People employ different ways of assigning validity or of measuring the degree of truth in some conclusion, observation, or "fact." . . . What it amounts to is the belief by many that a great deal of the difficulty in getting a group to come to grips with a complex problem in a collective manner is that members of the group will often take very different views on the nature of "truth" or validity for a given "fact." This is further complicated when these fundamental differences in perspective are not recognized at the conscious level. It is therefore necessary to evolve communication structures that will promote the exposure of differences that exist at fundamental levels"

One practice trend that emphasizes a noun-perspective is the of electronic discussion groups in terms of "channels" and "effects." A host of studies have been published comparing computer-mediated communication to face-to-face (FtF) communication. One approach emphasizes the extent to which electronic discussion groups (EDGs) contribute to feelings of social presence among participants. Other researchers look at how the reduction of non-verbal channels in computer mediated communication (CMC) — the "cues filtered out" approach — impacts computer mediated communication (CMC) effectiveness.

Researchers often say that users compensate by developing alternative behaviours: typing emotional cues/ "graphic accents" on the screen; using emoticons, etc. Such practice has led to the development of the "media richness" hypothesis: that the unique characteristics of each communications medium contribute in different ways to the effective transmission of different types of messages. Walther comments that computer mediated communication (CMC) is a "lean" medium that best conveys "simple or unequivocal" messages; more complex messages, however, should be sent using "richer" media (e.g., face-to-face).

Other scholars focus on how the reduction in non-verbal information results in various forms of aggressive behaviour, including flaming, excessive swearing, name calling, insults, threats, or even "virtual rapes" notes that "[a]rgumentative exchanges among net group members are quite prevalent. The intensity and deviancy of such disembodied exchanges can become . . . heated and destructive . . .".

Other experiments emphasizing a noun-perspective focus on computer-mediated communication diffusion, usually within organizational settings. Social influence theory suggests that manager or peer attitudes can greatly impact computer mediated communication (CMC) diffusion. A related set of studies have focused on the use of group decision support systems (GDSS) to facilitate group collaboration.

One noun-oriented trend emphases the phases of group decision-making. For example, Hiltz and Turoff identified four general electronic discussion group (EDG)phases: creativity/ exploration — when participants brainstorm to generate the maximum number of alternative proposals; evaluation/consensus — when members debate the merits and deficiencies of the most salient proposals; model formation — when participants determine key relationships between the proposals; and comprehension/ decision — when members reach their final decision.

Other researchers have studied how channel or demographic predictors explain group outcomes. Olaniran found that mixed group decision support systems/face-to-face groups produced the highest quality decisions — although group decision support systems (GDSS) participants needed more time to complete decision tasks— and group decision support systems (GDSS) users generated the greatest number of brainstorming alternatives.

Likewise, prominent ritual/cultural approaches emphasize the nouns of communication within electronic discussion group (EDG) environments. For example, ethnographers often focus on a) user selection of nicknames or message topics or b) adoption/abuse of socially sanctioned rules, roles, and relationships when participating in online communities. An online fan community, "tools for the maintenance of intimacy, behavioral norms, and values have been developed by Phish.netters in a simultaneous attempt to contract and expand the community". Some argues that computer mediated communication (CMC) users "promote cultural understandings through the creation of commonly understood ways of symbolizing social and emotional contexts"

Thus, it is not surprising that electronic discussion group focuses on message threads, shared interests or feelings, identities, power relations, roles, social formations, or other noun-oriented characteristics of online communities. Left implicit is the actual process of how online participants construct the "sense of community" that is focus of so much research; actual human sense-making is often downplayed. Yet it is through sense-making moves that users ultimately constitute the sense of community.

Thus, what is needed is the explicit choice of a communication theory that acknowledges human sense-making of computer-mediated communication-based communities. Such an approach would explore dialogic rather than transmissional/cultural aspects of online communication — focusing on the verbs of communicative processes, the iterative step-takings of online participants as they "create, maintain, reify, destroy and reinvent structures".

Sense-Making Methodology provides a framework for explicating the process of community-building in online discussion groups. Dervin and others argues that a fundamental condition of human existence is a universal mandate to bridge gaps. Gaps exist within individuals (e.g., between head and heart, heart and hand), between and among people, between people and material objects, and between objects across time and space — assuming an epistemology and ontology that are in part both gappy and complete. As humans move through time and space, they continually build conceptual, emotional, or spiritual bridges (e.g, knowledge, understanding, sense, feelings) over the gaps they face.

Humans are conceptualized as social theorists, self-reflexively enlarging their repertoire of practices, behaviors, and thoughts as they bridge gaps. Since no two meaning-making moves can be exactly the same — time and/or space has shifted between one observation and the next — humans rely upon internal and external dialogues in order to triangulate their observations and make sense of their experiences. As Dervin et al. note, this dialogic process is central to human sense-making: "Dialogue involves iterative step-takings, an on-going never-ending bridging of order and chaos. Participants in communication are separated by gaps. Gaps are bridged through behavior. Some form of energy bridges these gaps. This bridging is done through the processes that these verbs of communicating represent—thinkings, listenings, observings, speakings", etc.

Applied to the online communities, Sense-Making Methodology suggests that any sense of community that emerges within online discussion groups would be the result of the sense-making moves made by humans continuously bridging gaps; attempts to label/identify/ online communities from the perspective of authority (e.g., the academic discourse surrounding computer mediated communication (CMC)) should be tempered/humbled by the voice of users struggling to make sense out of their online experiencings.

Typically, Sense-Making, employ an analytical triangle focusing on human situations, gaps, and uses. Situations are defined as the situation movement state that has led a human to a particular gap; to study this, the researcher asks the respondent to describe the situation that has led him to a time-space-bound episode. A respondent might point out that after having lost his job and home, he was forced to live on the street. Then, the respondent is asked to describe any questions he may have had in this situation: these questions help the identify the dimensions of the gaps faced.

Finally, the respondent describes the uses he received by way of answers to his questions; these help the examine the person's conceptual bridgings — the sense made or unmade — within the specified situation. A respondent might report finding a church-run mission, where he was given a meal, shower, and a place to spend the night.

The data collected — the respondent's verbal reports of situation-gap-use episodes — are then analyzed according to coding schemes developed by Dervin. The goal is to inductively identify verbing practices that explain the respondent's sense-making moves within the specified times-space bound contexts. Once identified, the examines these practices for patterns of structural production/ reproduction. It is these patterns — identified inductively by examining human sense-making moves — that may best explain how humans make/unmake sense in online environments.

In order to identify verbing practices within computer mediated communication (CMC)s, students in three communication classes were asked to take part in online discussion groups designed to supplement face-to-face class meetings. A total of 90 students — mostly undergraduate communication majors — participated in the electronic discussion groups (EDGs), each lasting from six to ten weeks. The students were asked to contribute at least two posts each week— using a self-chosen pen name or their real name—on topics related to class discussions and readings. To tap the human situations-gaps-uses of online sense-making, students were asked to describe the circumstances that led to each posting.

The unit of analysis was the student's self-report associated with the posting. User reports were coded for verbings according to a content analysis scheme suggested by Dervin and Dervin and Clark. As part of this analysis, each verbing was also examined according to relational "situation defining strategies" suggested by Dervin and Clark: individuals relating to self, individuals relating to other individuals, or individuals relating to collectivities.

The majority of postings — thirty one percent — related to human sharing of insight or pleasure. Of the rest, sixteen percent involved users praising others; fourteen percent related to students making connections between course or electronic discussion group (EDG) material; another thirteen percent involved users sharing their struggles with the group. An additional eleven percent of the verbings involved students relating similar experiences to those discussed in class or other entries, while the remaining fifteen percent involved users asking a question or asking for help, seeing contests between ideas, connecting with others, pointing out the cause of some phenomenon, or expressing a need for support.

Preliminary findings have uncovered an interesting pattern in the data: many of the messages were not responded to by others. In traditional computer mediated communication (CMC) analyses — where thread length is the operational definition for online communities, such postings would be coded as non-dialogic, not contributing to community formation. However, by examining these "solo" postings for verbing processes, sense-making tactics are uncovered showing users actively engaged in moments of community-constructings, or community-ings.

Further, as suggested by Dervin and Clark, a focus on verbings in which users relate self to self helps to identify sense-making moments that may also contribute to community-ing. Such moments seem to represent situations when users need to be listened to, whether or not someone else responds — suggesting the application of the talking cure.

Thus, coding these discussion entries in terms of verbing behavior helps us identify and analyze the sense-making activity happening within the electronic discussion group (EDG). Rather than categorizing postings as "main topics" or "responses" arranged in subject-driven "threads," they are examined for evidence of human sense-making activity — the verbs of communicative processes. As these examples have shown, postings that might otherwise be coded as not contributing to community-building can be reexamined under a much wider, more human lens, shedding light on communicative activity through which users actively make sense of their experiences as part of an online community.

The form and function of online communities has exploded during the past two decades. Typically, computer mediated communication (CMC)-oriented practice adopts either a transmission or ritual/cultural theoretical perspective that emphasizes the nouns of communication rather than the verbs of communicating.

The goal would be to develop truly responsive systems that assist users in making sense of their online experiences rather than privileging designer motives and agendas. As Dervin asserts, "such systems would be recursive and responsive at their core. Incorporating users would not be an afterthought, a focus of feedback and accountability studies, or even of formative evaluation studies. Users and all relevant constituencies would be defined into the heart of the system"

In practical terms, this means re-thinking system-based or designer-based categories —threads, topic lines, hits, roles, etc. — in favor of those derived from actual human sense-making tactics —sharing ideas or pleasure, praising others, seeing connections, sharing struggles, etc.

Second, an emphasis on communication as verb may lead to the development of more useful theory for explicating online dialogue and community-building than has been the case so far. The verbing approach encourages of communication as human process that changes from moment to moment and space to space. Rather than suggesting that such processes are too numerous and complex to practice, this has begun to show how the application of Sense-Making Methodology can lead to the development of theoretical taxonomies — even at this preliminary stage — that can advance understanding about communicative processes that lie at the heart of online community-building.

Thus, although much more work needs to be done in the application of Sense-Making Methodology to practice of online communities, the benefit of this approach is that it allows researchers to interrogate the received wisdom about the nature, form, and transmissional processes of online communities by highlighting user sense-making tactics within electronic discussion groups (EDGs). By explicitly examining user verbings, one can isolate and examine sense-making movements that contribute to the construction of online communities, allowing us to move from the communities to community-ings.

Diversity in On-line Discussions

The emergence of a global information infrastructure (GII) has created more opportunities for multicultural communication in the form of "online communities." By their nature these communities are as diverse as the technologies of the GII. A commonly held belief is that these on-line communities are also naturally democratic and open. As a result, important issues are being raised concerning how these different groups are coping with new technologies and what role factors such as gender and culture play in participation in and creation of these new systems.

The Internet draws together people of different cultural groups, both locally and around the world. There is a problem, however, with the predominant models of policy which assume that democratic participation in networked systems simply comes from the equal availability of technology and the necessary skills to access these systems. Instead, we have seen that even with the most basic of systems, women and minorities are not participating in anywhere near equal numbers. Consequently, a key goal of this area must be to inform the creation of policies to improve the equity of access and use of theses new technologies by all groups.

The primary focus of this practice, then, is how groups who are typically absent from these online communities, such as women and minorities, can participate more equally. This lack of participation in the GII has implications for the economic and social well-being of those excluded as well as for the larger global community. This work, therefore, also has implications at a global level as we look at the lack of participation of developing nations in the evolution of a global information infrastructure.

Cross-Cultural Comunication

Cross-cultural communication can be defined as consisting of intercultural, multi-domestic, and cross-gender communication or genderlect communication. Key issues in cross-cultural communication practice include styles of conflict and negotiation and construction of identity and self-disclosure in interpersonal and group contexts.

In cross-cultural communication, meaning and interpretations are derived both collectively and individually through inter action: collectively, in the sense that meanings are negotiated between communicators and, individually, because the process of interaction is mediated by individual perceptions that are subject to one's identity and expectations which are in turn guided by culture.

Thus, it may be argued that the culture in which norms are developed will be reflected in all interactions regardless of the communication medium. It has been widely recognized in cross-cultural practice that people der ive different meaning and often key information, however, from the contextual aspects of the interaction.

Consequently, it is critical to determine how such cultural norms affects communication processes in the context of mediated communication. Unfortunately, though, while there are significant bodies of practice on both intercultural and mediated communication, cross-cultural communication via electronic media has largely been overlooked.

High- and Low-Context and Communication

Based on his extensive study of cultures around the world, Hofstede identified four common dimensions upon which cultures could be compared: (i) power distance or the extent to which less powerful members of society accept that power is distributed unequally; (ii) masculinity or when there are clearly defined sex roles with male values of success, money and possessions as dominant; (iii) uncertainty avoidance or the extent to which people feel threatened by ambiguity; and (iv) individualism which reflects the relational ties between an individual and others. Although this practice focused on cultures of different nations, it can be argued that Hofstede's findings can also be applied to a variety of cross-cultural communication situations.

Scholars of cross-cultural communication, regard Hofstede's dimension of individualism as a crucial dimension of variability across cultures. It is also a key dimension in understanding interpersonal and group interaction and communication processes. In an individualistic culture, individuals are loosely integrated with others and values their own self interest and that of their immediate family only. In contrast, in collectivistic cultures, individuals re late to larger collectivities and groupings and themselves as integrated with the whole.

Hall describes cultures as being high- or low-context, with context serving as the information that surrounds and gives meaning to an event. In other words, in high-context cultures, meaning is found in the nature of the situation and relationships, while in low-context cultures meaning is found in the words.

Furthermore, key to interpersonal and communication behavior, high-context cultures strive for subtlety, patience and empathy, while low-context cultures value straight talk, assertiveness an d honesty. Hall explains that high-context cultures also value collective needs and goals and create "us-them" categories, while low-context cultures value individual needs and goals and believe that every individual is unique.

Ting-Toomey has developed Face-Negotiation Theory to explain cultural differences in a key communication context, negotiation and conflict. Her basic assumption is that all people negotiate face, with face serving as a metaphor for public self-image. Face Work involves enactment of face strategies, verbal and non verbal moves, self-presentation acts, and impression management interaction. Identity can always be called into question and this leads to conflict and vulnerability; however, this varies from culture to culture, particularly along the dimension of high- and low-context cultures.

Ting-Toomey describes this issue of identity and vulnerability in terms of the "faces of face." In high-context cultures one strives to preserve the other s autonomy through face-saving and to include the other through face-giving, while in low-context cultures, one seeks to preserve one's own autonomy through face-restoration and to include oneself through face-assertion. In conflict resolution and negotiation, communication styles vary based on concern for self- and other-face.

Gender and Communication

Some believes that gender differences can also best be observed from a cross-cultural approach, one that does not assume that differences arise from men's efforts to dominate women. The belief that masculine and feminine styles of discourse are best viewed as two distinct cultural dialects rather than as inferior or superior ways of speaking, typifies this stance and is summed up by the term genderlect. While some scholars do not believe that identifying gendered communication styles is important or even appropriate.

A significant body of fundamental issue of gender differences and communication practices exists. However, we need to refocus this practice away from a conceptualization of gender as an individual attribute to bring more attention to the structures of the relationship between gender and power.

A common perception, however, is that women talk more than men. For instance, practice has shown that men talk more in formal versus informal tasks and more in public versus private communication. The effect is that while same sex task teams produce consistent amount of output, in mixed sex teams, the men produce more than the women.

In public spaces, for instance, men speak for a greater length of time and men's speech is more on task while women's is more reinforcing. Men's talk serves to hold floor for extended lengths of time, so that talking exercises dominance and prevents others from speaking. The ultimate effect is a lack of regard for women and their speech. This dominance also implies higher social status and that men are more competent to complete the tasks or to the issues at hand than are women. There are obvious implications for women, then, as they are increasingly participating in public arenas such as the workplace and politics where they may not have equal opportunity for participation.

Women also strive less actively for control, whereas societal expectations are that men will dominate task-oriented discussions. This conversation dominance is evidenced by amount of communication, amount of interruptions with male dominance in speaking time achieved through interruptions. Some believes that this control of the interpretive control and goes beyond the genderlect.

Tannen states that while scholars recognize intuitively that interruption and topic control in conversation is encouraged by, and encourages, power imbalance, practice has shown that women actually interrupt more. She admits that this finding was puzzling until still other pracitce showed that there was, in fact, a difference in the patterns of interruption.

For instance, men raise more new topics than women and use interruptions to change subject and take floor, while women use interruptions as c ooperative overlap and to show support for the speaker. Tannen also identifies another key difference in the communication practices of men and women, i.e., men use a more adversarial style in discussions, while women are likely to ask more questions. Women also use verb qualifiers and have a pattern of politeness behaviors, leading to image of less intelligence.

Men also value freedom from censorship along with candor and debate and will violate negative politeness (i.e., imposition) with the longest posts, copying most text and the longest signature files. Women value harmony and will avoid conflict, controlling action to minimize damage, which is a positive politeness pattern.

Typically it is the most dominant and powerful group whose values take on a normative status. Herring contends that the issue then is to understand whose values inform the rules of behavior on the Internet. These differences that reproduce patterns of dominance must be known and understood in order that we may address them to achieve a more equitable and hospitable environment in cyberspace.

Listservs are only one form of on-line communication and are used for maintaining of email-based distribution lists on the Internet. Anyone who can send and receive Internet e-mail can access a listserv depending on its owner's permission. To subscribe to the listserv a potential user needs only to send an e-mail message to the listserv system. The listserv studied here was set up for graduate and undergraduate students enrolled in a global telecommunications course at a major urban university in the United States.

Other purposes of this implementation were also to explore the feasibility of listserv for enhancing the live classroom experience—with the possibility of using this technology as one component of a distance learning environment, as well as to evaluate more closely the characteristics and effectiveness of the group discussion process using this technology. This listserv was intended to create an open dialogue on topics related to the class. However, showing the tendency of a small group of individuals to dominate listserv discussions, the instructor established "netiquette" or guidelines for communication behavior in the discussion. These guidelines included: no flaming, no shouting, no personal messages, and no really long messages.

Topics were generally raised by the students and were related to the course material in global telecommunications. In addition, the graduate students were given the additional responsibility of keeping meaningful discussion going on the listserv. The topics addressed the impact of technology around the world from social as well as political and economic perspectives, and issues of cultural diversity and gender featured prominently in many of the discussions.

Implications

Some striking differences in communication patterns were observed on this listserv Ñ by gender and by culture and perhaps there was also an interaction between culture and gender. The magnitude of these differences is particularly noteworthy, since they occurred despite the instructor's efforts to create an open, free-flowing communication environment. These differences in communication patterns can be interpreted based on the systematic linguistic differences attributable to gender and culture.

In other words, these patterns of communication on the listserv could be said to simply be replicating patterns of interaction that are seen in traditional face-to-face situations. These patterns don't simply mirror traditional communication environments, where males dominate females and white American culture dominates others.

There are protections afforded in those traditional face-to-face channels of communication. In fact, some Net-watchers have observed that stripped of the social courtesies and contextual factors of traditional communication channels, this emerging communication environment is likely to be a less hospitable one than face-to-face.

Consequently, more than replicating traditional imbalances in communication practice, this new environment also may not comfortable for non-white, non-Americans, or females owing to its lack of contextual factors. In other words, the Internet may by nature be most conducive to the low-context culture of Western male society.

To this point, it is worth noticing that the African American women participated more in class than online. In fact, one of the African American women never joined the list and two only sent one message each. However, those women regularly come to class and two of them participated actively in class discussion. One of the observers remarked that it was if they felt "protected" in the classroom situation. This disparity in mediated communication environments has clear im plications, then, as an increasing amount of business, educational and even personal communication is mediated.

While the lack of non-verbal cues is worthy of further examination, an even larger question emerges: Is this technology actually fashioned after the values and perspectives of those who have created it. In the case of networked communication systems, the technology appears to be based on the dominant masculine value systems of

Western society. In addition, there is different access to the creation of the technology as well; and the result has been the creation of a place were social practices extend the asymmetrical construction of power.

With the growing use of computers, video games, and the Net, we may have a generation of children emerging within where everyone is equally comfortable in that environment. Also, the technology is changing rapidly, with dramatic increases in channel capacity, allowing for more and different cues to be included in the communication process. However, as the Net becomes "tiered", only some individuals will have access to this greater speed and broadband capacity, and the implications for those already under represented in those networked environments are enormous. Will they have the "left-over" old Net, or will they have the Super New Net that will allow them to have instant images, sound É maybe even touch and smell?

Perhaps the greatest implication is that in the near future, it is that the Net is still dominated in both academe and the business world by the discourse patterns of the dominant white male society, so that those women and men who want to participate equally, in the fullest sense will have to use the dominant patterns in order to "market" themselves. There are implications for policy from the most basic lev els involving civility in the classrooms to the development and deployment of the GII.

While there is widespread recognition of the impact of new information technologies on individuals, institutions and society, there is little consensus on what that impact is and how and whether there should be remediation. However, that there is an information or technology gap is indisputable—and these obstacles to equity in information technology exist, most specifically for women, minorities and the poor.

4

Electronic Media and Civil Society

Computer-mediated communication in sociology, philosophy and media theory, would like to comment on a polarization between two different "parties". One side can be characterized by the assumption that computer-mediated communication will lead to a further segmentation and fragmentation of our culture, because the structure of the Net and the way in which it is used reflects the different needs of various milieus, subgroups and individuals, and therefore encourage current tendencies of social and political disintegration. The other side emphasizes the democratic potential of Net media.

According to this more optimistic interpretation, the Internet may strengthen the position of citizens in relation to political authorities by allowing them to participate directly in political decision-making. This view emphasizes free access to information, globalization and lack of censorship as central characteristics of the Internet. Accordingly, electronic communication may introduce a new form of direct or plebiscitarian democracy because it seems to introduce new forms of participation, equality and social bonding. As a result, many theoreticians argue that in the long run, traditional mass media will be replaced by the Internet. They believe the Internet, by allowing direct contact between citizens and political representatives, will lead to a new form of public opinion which is no longer controlled by a few agents.

Position lies in between these two points of view. Referring to both theoretical and early empirical investigations, assume that electronic media will certainly change political public opinion, but in ways that are supplementary to existing forms of public communication. In particular that by virtue of its interactive communication structure the Internet may support the domain of public communication, which has been described as "civil society" in the context of theoretical discussion about democracy.

In this context, "civil society" refers to a network of civil activities and assemblies as well as social movements and pressure groups. These movements form an alternative public opinion, from which both political decisions and public opinion established by mass media proceed. So, civil society generates partial forms of public opinion which are relatively open, close to the needs of citizens and which are characterized by rather elaborate levels of discussion.

Relationship between Politics and Public Opinion

Modern societies have to be described as functionally differentiated societies. So meaningful structures, which are still connected to each other in premodern societies, have been separated from each other, and independent structures and functional systems have emerged. But the differentiation of society has not only improved its efficiency: it has also generated problems. The autonomy and closed character of the different functional systems not only imply opacity between systems because of the high inner complexity of each system; observe that systems ignore possible consequences of their own behaviour regarding other systems. As a result, modern societies are always confronted with problems of integration, unification and self-description. Here, the political system manifests some particularities.

On the one hand, as an autonomous system, it has the same characteristics and problems as any other functional system. But on the other hand, the political system has to find methods of integrating different perspectives in order to guarantee the consistency of a society. The political system must cluster the different perspectives of the functional systems within a society to generate a transcontextual consensus. And only the political system is seen as the legitimate system for formulating general rules and frameworks for other systems of society.

In looking for institutions that enable a society to find this kind of transcontextual agreement, public communication structures seem to play a fundamental role. On the one hand, they comment on political decisions and explain them to the citizens; on the other hand, they collect expectations and demands of the citizens and present them to the political system. Hence, political public opinion may be regarded as a communication system which mediates between the citizens and the political system by reciprocally selecting and transferring information.

Mass Media and Electronic Communication Networks

According to Gerhards and Neidhardt, the concept of political public opinion refers to different domains of public communication connected to each other. Every kind of public opinion involves opacities as well as discoveries of new forms of perceiving and constructing reality. Through particular ways of selecting, codification and re-codification, media generate new ways of world-making as well as areas of blindness. Neidhardt and Gerhards distinguish between three different forms of public opinion: public opinion grounded on interaction; public opinion based on assemblies; and public opinion generated by mass media. Each kind of public opinion implies specific ways of selecting, clustering and spreading information. The possible form of public opinion as based on interactive media in relation to public opinion based on mass media.

The functional differentiation of modern societies implies a plurality and multiplicity of different perspectives and ways of world-making. Therefore, modern societies can be compared to a chaotic field. So, every partial system must not only eliminate its internal complexity, but also determine its relationship to its environment as well as define its limits. This is especially true for the political system that is confronted with manifold expectations as developed by other functional systems. To eliminate this complexity, political systems have to develop strategies for selecting themes and topics.

Considering this problem, some suggests understanding public opinion as a mechanism for preselecting relevant themes and reducing complexity by generating particular techniques to filter information. In particular, mass media has undertaken this function and has even institutionalized it. Journalists select and prepare information and themes by following particular criteria that prevent them from presenting everything as they focus on particular topics. Besides, access to mass media is not straightforward. Institutions and organized actors find fewer obstacles to expressing themselves in mass media than single and non-organized actors. The possibility of rising to speak in mass media is not egalitarian - that is to say, relatively few people can influence this kind of public opinion.

In addition to this, producers and consumers are clearly separated in mass media, because the recipient is reduced to a passive role. Public opinion, generated by mass media, is not based upon the direct participation of citizens but on centralized ways of selecting information and focussing on specific topics. The influence of citizens on the generation of public opinion is more indirect and can often only be realized in restricted forms such as readers' letters.

In contrast to this, new electronic media can be characterized by high diversity and plurality of themes. A priori, no topic is excluded. Furthermore, there exist neither any criteria for preselecting information on the Net nor an efficient control of themes, except on the level of particular newsgroups and mailing lists. Therefore, electronic communication is comparable to a pool of information and topics without limits and without any centralized structure.

Furthermore, the access to the Net is rather open. People who want to discuss a topic can introduce themselves on the Net by presenting their ideas and suggesting a discussion about them. So, it is not only possible to get any information from the Net suitable for decision-making or other activities, but furthermore, people may participate in chat groups and propose for discussion personal viewpoints and particular arguments.

According to this the Internet is much more capable of considering the various demands and diverse interests of individual citizens than centralized, organized mass media. The individuals or participants of the public, who have been forced to take a passive consumer position in the era of mass media, can now articulate themselves and are in the position of generating a new foundation of political and public opinion, in contrast with the more centralized orientation of old media.

Mass media can be characterized by a rather uniform language, or—as Neidhardt and Gerhard put it - public communication is the communication of lay people. It is neither a communication of experts nor private communication, because everything has to be presented in a way that the standard citizen can understand it. In this way, mass media is able to mediate between politics and citizens. According to this, mass media is always confronted with the problem of capturing the attention of consumers. In this domain, the consequence is stiff competition which has an egalitarian effect.

So, production techniques become more and more comparable to each other and the products correspond to each other more and more. So, the specific criteria and codes of mass media have generated a kind of public opinion that has become an autonomous functional system. In contrast with this, in electronic media may observe that a different kind of public opinion emerges which is characterized by a plurality of topics and themes and a strong variability of codes.

The Internet allows direct participation as well as the generation of new topics by every user. While mass media restricts the user to an "exit-option", the user of electronic media has also a "voice-option" — that is to say, he or she can articulate his or her own opinion about a selected theme. The contribution of somebody is part of the message of the medium. Furthermore, there is at present no censorship on the Net. So, everybody can present his or her points of view in his or her own language, which is separate from the censored and generalized code which regulates the way how information is to be presented in mass media.

The difference between the balcony and the stage - to say it metaphorically - which characterizes mass media, does not exist in electronic media because everybody can participate in the process of producing, selecting and spreading information. Accordingly, the Internet supports the diversity of languages and topics, and its interactive structure helps to overcome the traditional dualism of producer and consumer.

But on the other hand, this diversity of themes and languages generates some basic problems. On the Net, it is rather difficult to find a kind of common language that would enable participants to focus on central problems. The Internet may be regarded as a kind of stage for particular interests and identities, but it is no medium in which to express and develop global political strategies and negotiate common standards for talking together.

Primarily, there is no "the citizen" who is discussing with other citizens on the Net. Rather, there are simply individuals - such as experts, old people, homosexuals, women, men, children, youngsters - who debate their particular interests on the Net. Hence, electronic media underlines the internal differentiation of society by generating polycontextural communication structures. So, the electronic communication on the Net may be regarded as an example of a postmodern culture of communication.

Statements about the function of mass media concerning their way of distributing information are controversial. Positions based on system theory claim that public opinion is established by mass media, because mass media reports on political events by taking the position of a gatekeeper and controlling what will be presented and what will be hidden. So, every political actor sees what political action has been considered as relevant and what effects on other political actors can be observed. Furthermore, according to system theory, processes of selecting and filtering information and presenting relevant topics to political discussion should be regarded as the second important function of mass media.

Other models describing the function of mass media surmount these ideas, according to which the main function of mass media can be described as a selection task. According to this more elaborate position, public opinion can only fulfill its social, cultural and political function if it takes into account the perspectives of all representatives within a society.

Furthermore, the interests and topics of these different representatives have to follow discursive standards of communication, so that they may lead to rational and reasonable insights, problem-solving strategies and perspectives, which can be addressed politically. Considering the effect of electronic media from this point of view, it still seems rather unclear as to which relationship exists between communications strategies on the Net and political decision-making. Electronic media will influence the structures and the function of mass media.

Looking at the media theory, often find euphoric hopes and visions concerning the political effect of new media. So it is argued that the Internet may generate more transparency in political processes and that citizens may become more involved in political decisions. Following this, modifications of political public opinion are expected. On the one hand, it is assumed, that mass media will be replaced by the Internet; on the other hand, people think that the Net will supplement mass media by creating new spaces of public opinion.

The electronic media will not replace mass media. The specific power of mass media is due to its capacity to motivate political actors to become interested in specific themes. According to this, theoreticians refer to the mobilizing function of mass media. In contrast with this, the Net lacks the ability to dramatize problems in a way that political systems must take care of them.

On the Net, there is no strategy for clustering different perspectives and discourses so that they may represent transcontextual themes and perspectives and that they could be answered by political decisions. This is one of the main reasons why people often complain about the lack of order and orientation on the Net. So, at least for the moment, mass media cannot be replaced by electronic communication networks, as only mass media guarantees this kind of transcontextual clustering of topics and is able to force political reactions. But the Net enlarges the possibilities of citizens of articulating their interests. Considering this, the Net will influence political public opinion to a large extent, because new domains of discussion and new discourse forms will enlarge current ways of generating public opinion.

At this point, it seems appropriate to refer to Habermas, who distinguishes between a kind of general public opinion generated by mass media, and a different form of partial public opinion which is less formal. Partial public opinion is characterized by variable non-governmental and non-economical associations and assemblies. According to Habermas, these pre-institutional forms of public opinion often contradict general public opinion produced by mass media and form an important space of resonance for the problems and interests of citizens.

Mass media cannot exist without this foundation of deliberate associations, because otherwise, the formal structure and the clear professional separation between the producers and the auditorium would not be able to mediate between politics and citizens. Partial public opinion, like these non-formal associations, is more characterized by authenticity, creativity and sensibility; that is to say, partial public opinion is more open towards those problems and interests which are not represented in public opinion generated by mass media.

Following Habermas, partial public opinion has to intervene between the generalized and formal functional systems, on the one hand, and the vivid lifeworld of citizens, on the other hand. Social movements and community pressure groups lift up the concrete problems of citizens and present them to political institutions and their representatives.

Public opinion which is produced by such informal groups is not only a very important indicator of whether the system as a whole is functioning; furthermore, here exists a vivid power of innovation, critique and creativity through presenting different perspectives to political institutions and through considering the diversity of various viewpoints. These associations and movements, this kind of partial public opinion, will profit from electronic communication. Such communication presents the opportunity to be engaged in such discourses, an extensive plurality and diversity of perspectives and ideas, and an openness and freedom in these communication environments as lacking - at the time of this writing - a restrictive censorship. Taking all this into account, the processes on the Net seem to be comparable to communication structures of pre- institutional alternative public opinion.

Accordingly, the Internet could intensify and enlarge the relationship between general public opinion and private milieus and individual lifeworlds. This may strengthen the signal function of public communication. Some examples, like the accident in Chernobyl, the Gulf war or the civil war in the former Yugoslavia, are interesting indicators of such a form of alternative public opinion. But, this rather optimistic assumption concerning the social benefit of interactive media is confronted by some fundamental problems, which may limit the signal function of computer-mediated communication. So, it is possible to argue against our interpretation by considering that even in industrialized countries, only a very small part of the population has access to the Internet.

For many people, the personal computer and related equipment which would enable them to participate in on-line discussions is still too expensive. And in countries of the so-called "third world," the situation is even worse: most of the inhabitants of these countries do not even have a telephone connection. Therefore, the possibility of participating in democratic decision-making processes is restricted to a very small, prosperous part of the population.

Another problem appears if consider that not only financial resources are a necessary precondition of participation: in addition, people should be endowed with so-called cultural capital. Studies of "net-surfers" have shown that most of the active users of the Internet not only possess sufficient money and technical competence, but also a specific educational and cultural background which includes competencies such as speaking English and being able to present arguments in a rational way. An active participation in on-line discussions presupposes the ability to overcome the shyness to articulate one's own opinion, to present arguments, and to deal with the anonymity of the communication situation. Taking this into account, to concede that, despite the growing number of Net users, it will be some time until the majority of the population will have learned to use the Net as a means of democratic participation.

The habit of the passive consumer, which people have achieved over many years of adopting traditional mass media, cannot be broken very quickly. So that moving from this passive role to an active user of interactive media is still in its beginning stages. Furthermore, it would be necessary to implement general social reforms to accelerate this process, because the structures of many political decision-making processes - for example the information flow between administration and citizens - would have to be modified to enable people to participate in these processes.

Another aspect which might limit the generation of civil society in the Internet is the fact that electronic communication very often either takes place in thematically restricted domains such as specific news-groups, or in environments like MOOs or MUDs which are more characterized by playful habits than by rational discourse strategies. So, looking at processes on the Net, seldom find discussions about global political perspectives and topics which are relevant to the society in general. Rather, participants concentrate on very particular themes and more private needs and interests. Often, they demarcate their activities from other groups by elaborating particular styles of communication and specific language codes. Because it is difficult to find transcontextual perspectives and themes, most of the participants are limited to their specific discourses and do not even try to make them available to public discussions.

Accordingly, it becomes more and more difficult to find general topics and a commonly shared foundation of perspectives and beliefs. The clustering of viewpoints and strategies is seldom found on the Net and general objectives are more and more replaced by individual interests. So, the rhizome-like structure of the Internet does not support the development of binding insights, gathering views, binding problem-solving strategies and common perspectives; rather, it supports particular orientations and the fragmentation of communication processes. Hence electronic communication fits in current trends of further segmentation of society, because it strengthens the dissemination of pluralistic and incommensurable discourses instead of supporting the generation of a commonly shared lifeworld.

At least we would like to point out that the early vision of the Internet as a free, anarchistic medium without a centralized structure is confronted by an opposing tendency. For some time, it has been observed that anarchistic, free and uncontrolled communication structures, which have been main characteristic of the Internet, are confronted by the development of new hierarchies, new centralized structures, and new ways of protecting, controlling and concealing information. Some theoreticians fear that the Internet is no longer a free and accessible communication environment.

According to initial studies, a tendency can be observed which shows a dichotomy between public and private channels on the Net. The public domain is accessible for every user, but only takes up rather unimportant information, while private channels, which are politically more relevant, are not accessible for everybody but only for a small group of responsible and powerful persons. The current discussion about governmental regulation of pornography also fits this tendency of establishing centralized structures of demarcation and exclusion.

The facts which call into question the view that the Internet can support the development of civil society must certainly be taken into account. The mixture of private and public communication which is typical for Net communication, as well as the thematic restrictions of online discussion groups and the fragmentation of communication culture, oppose the hope for discursive agreement on the Net.

On the other hand, the Net enables people to put forward every theme and every topic for discussion and to participate in any on-line-discussion group they choose. So the idea that the Internet supports the generation of a global communication society has to be replaced by the idea that public opinion on the Net is more characterized by pluralistic perspectives, an unlimited number of on-line discussions groups, and multiple connections between different "communication-arenas."

This pluralistic concept of public opinion is also confronted with the problems mentioned above. But as these problems could - at least to some extent - be overcome by social reforms and political support, it remains an open question whether the Net will support the generation of this kind of pluralistic public opinion. The Internet may function as an organ for pre-institutional organizations and for individuals. By this mean that it may take on a signal function for political decisions. Because of its interactive and rather decentralized structure, the Internet enables people to present their perspectives and positions in a still rather unlimited way. But we also know that social and political reforms have to be pushed forward to allow the development of an egalitarian access for everybody despite his or her social, ethnic and cultural background: otherwise, the vision of a civil society - supported by the Net - will remain a pure slogan.

Influence on Society

The media - television, radio, and newspapers, is the worlds' most powerful means of communication. The media has a strong impact on our lives. In many cases, what we see in the media is not the truth. What they show is one sided- they tell what they feel is the most important. Society is being brainwashed by what they see on television, hear on the radio and read in the newspaper. Both the gangsters of the past, and todays gangsters - gangsta rappers, can be viewed in both a negative and positive light.

India is a large and diverse country with an equally sizeable and varied media. The spurt of growth in this media has a tremendous impact on shaping development values as it informs, educates and entertains. Indian government tried to control airwaves but could not hold it for a long. Today Indian sky is flooded with several channels - both Indian (Doordarshan) as well as foreign. The foreign channels combine foreign programmes with indigenous ones. There is no direct control on them. This is very clear in their carrying commercials on alcohol and a large number of soap operas round the clock, which have very little relevance with the Indian society. However they try to project their sincerity by showing some token programming having developmental messages.

Doordarshan initially started with the goal of using television for development purpose has joined in a race with the foreign channels. As a result though there are more than 50 channels and round the clock transmission is available on Indian television the actual choice of viewing is not that wide. The choice is between one sitcom to the other of the same production teams whether it is Doordarshan or any other channel. In this situation it is difficult to expect attitudinal revolution on the part of the programme makers. As a result with the quantity of the programmes the quality (not technical) has hardly improved. The people are constantly exposed to the messages majority of which are basically from the commercial houses. Television is a major source of audio-visual images in developing countries. In general women are more regular in their television viewing compared to the men. The lower the income group, the more regular are viewers, both male and female, compared to the higher income groups.

Many viewers, especially women, seem to be compulsive viewers. Similar results were obtained in American society during '80s. Television is the people's medium and the one particularly relied upon by those who for reasons of education, income or culture, have limited access to or make little use of other sources - the poor, blacks and other minorities and the elderly. These groups voluntarily or involuntarily are dependent on television and a sizeable population is totally and involuntarily so". On the other hand in USA for the past ten years research has consistently come up with the same result that of male characters out-numbered female by two to one on television. Only a minority of the women portrayed is mature adults, compared to 70 percent of the men portrayed. Two out of three men are depicted in some occupational context compared to only two out of five women.

While the direction of media reform in India has often been viewed in the context of demand and supply, its exclusionary and piece meal characteristics would appear to have been relegated to the background. These have significant fall-outs in terms of media democratization in the country. Even a cursory look at the pace of decentralization would take cognizance of its selective and reactive characteristics. If the first is predictable under a 'market is the mantra' regime, the latter is worrying as it raises a larger question: Does the course of the reforms conform to a larger and cogent media policy, or are they symptomatic of a crisis - management and reactive culture?

While there are no easy answers, community would appear to have paid the heaviest price in an ambivalent and unlevelled media playing field. In a county of daunting socio-economic divides accompanied by a formidable diversity of languages, dialects and cultures, the potential for community media should have assumed critical significance. Unfortunately, the gap between potential and practices would appear to have widened, judged by the media trends. Community voices, if at all, struggle at the periphery of a contrasting and often iniquitous media landscape. In contrast to the government's efforts to bridge the digital divide and take information technology to the masses, the colonial and fossilised Indian Telegraph Act of 1885 continues to hold sway over the broadcasting arena. On the one hand, the Supreme Court Judgement of 1995 has endorsed that 'airwaves are public property.' However, in the practical realm, lines between public and privately remain conveniently blurred.

While Private Radio has made an entry into the Indian broadcast arena, community radio remains to find legitimacy by the law of the land, notwithstanding New Delhi's recent New Year gift enabling residential educational institutions to be eligible for 'campus community radio.' In terms of reach and access, India's print and broadcast media manifest - very substantially - the characteristics of mass media. 'While newspapers elsewhere struggle to hold readers, Indian daily circulation has increased by close to 500% in 20 years. Two all-India readership surveys conducted in 1999-2000, estimate that the press as a whole reaches between something 200 and 240 million persons. Translated in terms of percentages this means that about 60% of urban Indians and 25% of rural Indians read print media regularly. Radio's reach is even more comprehensive covering about 96% of the country. But, notwithstanding this growth in terms of reach, media's impact on development and governance remains, at best, tenuous.

In fact there would appear to remain a substantial gap between potential and experience. Paradoxically, in terms of need, the role of media in bridging the development gap is more keenly felt today than ever before. The 1990s, especially in the socio-economic context, yields a disquieting picture. Globalisation's impact on the poverty map leaves much to be desired. Even World Bank statistics point to a rise in the number of poor, with '40 million people' in India having joined their ranks during the 1990s. The latest Human Development Report statistics point to India slipping further down the ranks to stand at 127, three notches down from the previous year. The situation is elaborated by development economist and head, human development programme, National Council of Applied Economic Research, Abusaleh Shariff. In a recent interview he asserted that 'if the definition of poverty were expanded to incorporate the human development parameters, the world poverty level would touch 60%.' In the Indian context, '70% of our people will qualify as poor,' while the below poverty line figures indicated 26% to be 'worse than chronically poor.' Other observations and commentaries merely accentuate the argument.

India also enters the "millennium" with hundreds of millions of illiterates. Again, spending on education in India is less than 4% of GDP. Far less than the 6% that the government itself says is the minimum required. In terms of quality of life the picture is far from rosy. New nutritional data at the all India level show that average calorie intake declined steadily in both rural and urban areas between 1973 and 1994. The threat of political conflict, communalism and terrorism has also palpably impacted on the notion of a democratic nation state. The media's response to these trends has been a mixed bag. A study conducted by the Centre for Development and Learning, Bangalore, in 2000 focussed on media coverage of development issues in newspapers.

For instance, in the Times of India (one of the largest dailies in the country), 4% of a total of 24 pages were devoted to development news. This percentage proved to be more or less representative in terms of coverage in many other dailies.' Media's relationship with governance is equally tenuous. Media coverage of the recent communal strife in Gujarat has, in the main, been positive. But disparities do exist. As Mukul Sharma points out, 'both media and governance in India suffer from serious problems, which at times, even feed into each other. Suspension of civil liberties, excessive militarisation, communal assertions and homogenising tendencies have too often spelled doom for Indian democracy.

Media become more sensitive on issues of democratic governance, people's struggle against social injustice, and so on...' This, however, is only part of the picture. If the media are effectively to mirror society, then 'the role of people's organisations, social movements, voluntary organisations and other civil society formations in monitoring the functioning of the media and making it more people centred is critical.' It is here, that the rub comes. Unlike the government or political parties and sections of the corporate sector who have developed the own press and media channels, voluntary organisations, social groups and activists, have not been able to develop their own press and television channels in a sustained manner. The exceptions that exist are usually journals/newsletters of development organisations which cannot in terms of size or scope make a sustained dent at the macro level. What is required is an active tradition of community/peoples media.

The promise of media reform which gathered momentum in the 1980s and 90s unfortunately did not actualize into performance. The journey from the Broadcast Bill to the Convergence Bill generated considerable expectations in the public domain - only to fritter away into cynicism. While the Broadcast Bill suffered an untimely death, the Convergence Bill (notwithstanding the hype it initially evoked) remains to be tabled in the Lok Sabha despite the passage of three years. Clearly, an overt lesson would indicate a reluctance, at the policy level, to 'walk the talk'. This weakness in political will towards media reform per se becomes more evident in taking a closer look at broadcast legislation. The Prasar Bharati Act, which in many ways provides a watershed in media legislation in the country, demonstrates this substantially.

Role of Community Radio

One of the reasons cited by official quarters for the absence of community radio legislation is the lack of demand. While it is true that community radio advocacy needs to go beyond preaching to the converted, it is not realistic to restrict it to a clutch of initiatives any longer. Post New Delhi's campus radio initiative in early 2003, there have been several universities across the country which have not only evinced interest, but introduced community radio as a part of their media pedagogy. These include Anna University in Tamil Nadu, Indira Gandhi National Open University, Jamia Millia and the Indian Institute of Mass Communications in New Delhi. At the same time, several development NGOs at the grass roots level have initiated or facilitated endeavours which demonstrate community participation in radio. Notwithstanding the need for the recommendations to receive the official stamp of approval, their provisions palpably demonstrate the contrast between private and community broadcasting. These, in turn, effectively mirror the overall media climate in the country.

Communication includes all methods of disseminating information, knowledge, thought, attitudes, and beliefs. Modern mass media like newspapers, cinema, and television, and traditional media of social communication like the bazaar, puppet show, drama, dance, local meetings, as well as inter-personal communication media like posts and telegraphs, teleprinters, and telephones all impact language use. The underlying and basic factor of these categories of mass media is language. Hence for the effectual and proper utilisation of these mass media, language education is very essential and material. Interpersonal communication media helps meet the demand for mutual communication and exchange of information among people and institutions. In recent years, the use of computer has far reaching effect on language education and communication. In this field also language education is of paramount importance. The special feature of radio, television, and cinema is that they serve the needs of both literates and illiterates. They will also entertain people in remote areas not within the reach of newspapers. On the other hand, newspapers present the 'written word' and serve as 'record,' while at the same time give local coverage. Language education to the audience, readers and spectators is very essential.

In India, various forms of language are in competition with each other to draw the attention of the public. These forms range from the extremely informal style of speech found in the radio and the cinema to the formal styles found in newspapers and news broadcasts. Different language styles perform different functions in society. The styles of standard languages constantly undergo changes and development through the impact of various mass communication media. Formal public education is one of the most powerful tools that influences linguistic norms and linguistic attitudes. Another important aspect of language education in India is culture learning. One learns a language through being culturally aware. Thus there is interrelationship and reinforcement between language and culture. They are inter-dependent. News texts are part of what a particular culture thinks of as significant, and show a hierarchy of values.

The newspaper is 'talk' about world affairs and current events, having multifarious functions in society such as disseminating information, socialisation, motivation, education, cultural learning, entertainment, integration, etc. Most newspapers in Indian languages appear to focus on the readability of the material or news they present. They recognize that the way language is used is an important factor in enabling their readers to come back to them. But language alone does not help a newspaper to increase its sale in the market place. In a country where everything is looked at from a political angle, the support base for a newspaper in Indian languages often comes from the shades of political opinion that a newspaper supports and highlights.

The manner a news item is presented and highlighted depends on the "ideology" of the newspapers. This "ideology" controls and regulates language use. Of the different mass media, newspapers assume great importance as they deal every day with dissemination of current information pertaining to different aspects of human life, such as social, economic, political and cultural, both at national and international levels. In a newspaper, headlines occupy a prominent position by summarising the most important news of the day in a nutshell, which facilitates the reader with quick reading and comprehension.

The choice of expression plays a vital role in making the headlines more effective. Thus language plays a prominent part and it aims at educating the reader. At present Indian language newspapers show a tendency to use simpler and colloquial forms of expression more frequently. Newspapers in Indian languages at present have also begun to use loaded expressions with sarcasm and cynicism, because the growing middle class around the nation that buys and reads the newspapers is basically cynical about politics and politicians. The newspapers are educators of the literate and not so literate public. Now-a-days newspaper reading habit is growing rapidly and widely. Thus there is the steady and expanding process of language education through newspapers. The educated families in south India a generation ago made it a point to read THE HINDU daily newspaper as part of their daily English education.

History reveals that the Press Acts against vernacular press in British India actually helped the people to seek greater freedom and ultimately independence from Britain. Political, social, and economic revolutions in India are closely related to the active involvement and development of newspapers in Indian languages. The prose of every Indian language is critically developed and guided by the language style used in the newspapers published in these languages. In order to establish their own identity, newspapers deliberately coin and choose their own language expressions. For example, there is a great tendency these days to combine various native words with English words to create special expressions. Translation is no more a fashion with most Indian languages newspapers. Some thirty years ago, most Indian languages newspapers made special effort to translate words and phrases in to Indian languages. Now they tend to simply transcribe foreign words in the native script. This tendency is supported by the spread of cable TV as well as by the globalization process.

Further in a democratic country like India, the newspaper acts as a powerful weapon in exposing the irregularities, shortcomings, and failures of government policy and also function as an eye-opener of the public. But newspapers should not abuse their status and functions. They should be above bias and should be fair and impartial. The language used should be of high standard aiming at educating the public not only in terms of news content but also in terms of language use. This twin function is not wholly appreciated or even discerned in some newspapers that seek only sensationalism in content and expression.

Radio has greater potential in mass communication than the newspaper for two reasons. Firstly, it reaches even the remote corners of the country and has no physical impediments. Secondly, it imparts language education and provides entertainment and disseminates information to both literate and illiterate listeners. Radio is under government control for fear of its misuse and powerful influence. There are indications that soon we will have privately owned radio stations with their own programs of broadcasts all over the country. The range of programmes includes a wide variety of educational, cultural and entertainment items, aimed at a broad spectrum of classes of people.

The type of language used in government-controlled radio stations, unfortunately, seems to be artificial in its idiom in the broadcasts done in all Indian languages. The broadcasts for farmers and workers try to use a style that is supposedly understood by less literate groups. We are yet to find a balance in the broadcasts that suit the audience for which these are intended. But the broadcasts are not as appropriate as these should be for the simple reason that these broadcasts are still largely government-controlled. Radio has a major role to play in language.

The language used in radio impacted the previous generation very much. News broadcasts introduced chaste language, closely modelled after the written variety. The newsreaders introduced standard pronunciation values to the phonemes, words, phrases, and sentences. The impact of radio language was heavy upon the written style, rather than on the spoken idiom. This is somewhat strange, considering the fact that radio is mainly an audio form. It appears that Indian radio is more closely associated with news and music than with dialogue. Television is the audio-visual non-literary media having the additional advantage of being able to use visual cues to reinforce the information being presented in spoken form. Thus even in this field language education plays a vital role, because additional cues compensate for dialectal differences between speakers and hearers.

The potential of television as an educative device is very great. But exploiting this potential depends upon the choice of appropriate language. TV programs are telecast through satellites. The satellite TV offers a dazzling array of channels and programme choices in many different languages. The divide between the literate and less literate or non-literate classes is covered up in the television media. Media discourse provides a fertile ground for traditional cultural learning, even as it provides opportunities to entertain and educate the viewers in novel and wholly modern ways that work against traditional values. Unfortunately, TV is more cinema-centered than radio. Entertainment takes precedence in TV. The impact of TV on Indian languages, in terms of their lexicon and structure, so far seems to be negligible. Privately owned TV channels often follow the models set by the leading newspapers in their coverage. The language of cinema, on the whole, is more accessible to the average person than that of other media.

The movies, in general, make use of colloquial style of speech. The language of the cinema, like that of other media, also shows considerable variation. The cinema, being closer to informal popular speech, has two advantages: 1. It appeals to mass audience, and 2. it portrays everyday situations wherein popular language is more appropriate than the more formal variety. In the village context the cinema competes with other forms of entertainment because it assesses a more popular language. There is, however, a serious problem. Until early seventies, most movies in Indian languages often followed a style that was closer to the written style. These days, movies are produced mostly in the colloquial idiom, except those movies that try to depict the heritage through mythology, etc. A movie viewer does not get introduced to the written variety now a day. Since in many Indian languages the distinction between the formal and informal styles of language or the distinction between the colloquial/spoken and written styles are still maintained, the usefulness of watching a movie in order to improve the competence in mother tongue is practically less significant.

Ongoing Computer Revolution

The computer Revolution in teaching Indian languages is still not yet widespread, despite the fact that computer software engineering is the most preferred profession for the educated young men and women in India. Driven by economic pursuits and greed, Indians seem to be competing with one another in offering their services to enrich the already rich nations. And yet, it is a fact that the presence of Indian languages in the world-wide-web is more significant than any other group of languages in the developing world. Certain Indian linguistic groups such as Kannadigas, Telugus, and Tamils seem to be more advanced in taking advantage of the computer revolution to improve their language education. There is a significant impact in language use brought out by the use of e-mail. Abbreviations even in Indian languages seem to be used more commonly these days. Once upon a time, inscriptions in copper plates and stones used abbreviations as a means to communicate information in short sentences, etc.

Time was not the main consideration when a few generations ago Indians used lots of abbreviations in spelling and combination of letters in their written documents. But, for this generation, time is an important consideration and they use abbreviations of different sorts in their e-mails, and chats. People want to be different from one another, especially from one generation to another. Wireless, cell phone abbreviations become the dominant feature of urban young men and women these days. Languages are mangled or deconstructed in an idiosyncratic manner. Indian languages find a significant place in the Unicode. This is a great contribution from the energetic Indian software engineers.

However, just like the technical terms created by committees constituted by various governments and their agencies, the use of Unicode characters allotted to Indian languages are not yet popular with the Indian public. Computers store material and keep them in memory. They express the correct use of language. They furnish valuable information concerning various subjects. They operate at high speed and provide opportunity for rectifying and correcting mistakes and errors. Thus the computer, mainly having literary merits, plays a very significant role in language education. It provides knowledge and information in almost all the major languages, both national and international.

The main projects that describe the growth of educational radio are:

School Broadcast Project: This project was commissioned in 1937 and the target group was School students. This programme started from Delhi, Calcutta, Madras and Bombay. In the beginning the school programme were not strictly governed by the curriculum. With the passages of time and acquisitions of more experience, the AIR tried to make its radio broadcasts more curriculum oriented, but in absence of common syllabi and time tables in schools, even within the same state, it could not succeed in it's aim.

Adult education and community development project (Radio Forum): Commenced in 1956, the Villagers of 144 villages in the vicinity of Poona (in Maharastra state), were the main beneficiaries of this project. This was agriculture-based project, which was originally designed and tried out in Canada. With the help of UNESCO, it was tried in 144 villages of Poona and was named as ' Radio forums Project' (defined as a listening cum-discussion-cum-action group). The members of the forum could listen thirty-minute radio programme on some agricultural or community - development programme, then discuss and decide regarding it's adoption in their own village. This project was a great success. Many action programmes were planned and put into practice.

Farm and Home Broadcast Project: This project was commenced in 1966 and again targeted at Farmers and villagers. These broadcasts were designed to provide information and advice on agricultural and allied topics. The aim was to educate the farmers and provide them assistance in adopting innovative practices in their fields as per the local relevance. The experts also conducted occasional farm radio schools, which proved to be very effective.

University broadcast project: This project for University students was initiated in 1965, with an aim to expand higher education as widely as possible among the different strata of society. The Programme consisted of two types- 'General' & 'enrichment'. The general programmes included topics of public interest and enrichment programmes supported correspondence education offered by universities in their respective jurisdictions. School of Correspondence studies, University of Delhi and the Central Institute of English and Foreign Languages, Hyderabad is well known for preparation and broadcast of their programmes through AIR.

Language Learning Programme: The project, popularly known as 'Radio Pilot project' was started in 1979-80 jointly by AIR and Department of Education Government of Rajasthan, with an aim to teach Hindi to School going children as first language in 500 primary schools of Jaipur & Ajmer districts on experimental basis. The project was found useful in improving the vocabulary of children. With its success, similar project was repeated in Hoshangabad district of Madhya Pradesh with some modifications but had limited success.

IGNOU-AIR Broadcast: In collaboration with IGNOU, AIR stations of Mumbai, Hyderabad and Shillong started radio broadcasts of IGNOU Programmes from January 1992.

Main target group of this project were students of Open / Conventional Universities. Although Shillong started this but discontinued later on. Therefore presently it is being broadcast from AIR Mumbai and AIR Hyderabad only. This programme is still popular in the respective region.

IGNOU-AIR Interactive Radio Counselling (IRC): Started in 1998 for students of Open / Conventional Universities, this project is also very successful. In order to bridge the gap between Institutions and learners by instantly responding to their queries and also to provide Academic Counselling in subject area, IGNOU in collaboration with AIR Bhopal started this project in May 1998 as an experimental programme for one year. With the success of the experiment, it was extended to 8 other AIR stations (Lucknow, Patna, Jaipur, Shimla, Rohtak, Jalandhra, Delhi and Jammu). Presently Interactive Radio counseling is being provided on every Sunday for one hour from 186 radio stations of All India Radio. This includes two Sundays on the National hook-up. Toll-free telephone facility is available from 80 cities enabling the learners to interact with experts and seek clarification, without paying for their telephone calls. The first and third Sundays of the month, AIR stations of Delhi (Hindi) and Kolkata (in English) broadcast from national hook-up, which 186 radio stations relay either of them. The 2nd and 4th Sunday are slotted for programmes of various regional centers of IGNOU and State Open universities respectively. The slot of 5th Sunday (if any) has also been given to region-based programmes of IGNOU. This programme is gaining popularity day by day.

Gyan-Vani (Educational FM Radio Channel of India): This project is recently launched (in year 2001) and again the target group is students of Open / Conventional Universities. Gyan Vani (Gyan = Knowledge, Vani = aerial broadcasting) is Educational FM Radio Channel of India, a unique decentralised concept of extending mass media for education and empowerment, suited to the educational needs of the local community. It is operating presently through Allahabad, Banglore and, Coimbatore FM stations of India on test transmission mode. The network is slotted to expand to a total of 40 stations by June-2002.

Gyan Vani stations will operate as media cooperatives, with day-to-day programmes contributed by different Educational Institutions, NGO's and national level institutions like IGNOU, NCERT, UGC, IIT, DEC etc. Each stations will have range of about 60-KM radius, covering the entire city /town plus the surrounding environs with extensive access. It serves as ideal medium addressing the local educational developmental and socio cultural needs (IGNOU, 2001). Gyan Vani is not only for the conventional educational system but also a main tool in making available the dream of education for all come true. Gyan Vani's main intention is to take education to the doorsteps of the people.

Gyan Vani, in addition to giving the hardcore education will also deal with awareness programmes including the ones for Panchayati Raj Functionaries, Women Empowerment, Consumer Rights, Human Rights, the Rights of the Child, Health Education, Science Education, Continuing Education, Extension Education, Vocational Education, Teacher Education, Non-formal Education, Adult Education, Education for the handicapped, Education for the down trodden, education for the tribals and so on. Gyan Vani is available through commercial FM radio set.

Radio-Vision (Multimedia through Digital Radio): Pioneered by the BBC, the technique of radio-vision allows the subject matter to be presented through two channels, the audio and the visual. The visuals are presented in the form of still filmstrips, charts, slides, models, etc, while the explanation is given through recorded narration. Educational institutions use this as a substitute for educational television. A small experiment in the use of radio-vision technique was carried out by The National Council of Education Training and Research, India in 1975-

76 using it as one of the components of the multi-media package for in service teacher training designed and operated during SITE. A series of charts and picture cards were presented to about 24,000 participating teachers 2400 centres alongwith verbal explanation provided through specially prepared radio broadcasts. The results were found to be encouraging.

A pilot project was carried out in IGNOU in 2001 under UNESCO support for testing the feasibility of using the new digital technology for cost effective transmission of audio-visual courseware. The project proved that FM Radio transmitters and Satellite Radio transponders can be used successfully to transmit, downlink and download multimedia courseware, in this case using the Asia Star of WorldSpace.

Radio-text: Radio has been used along with textual data transfer via computer networks simultaneously to create a 'radio-text' environment. The teaching end is normally a FM radio station having data broadcast facility through a computer network. The main points of the radio broadcast are sent through textual mode to the receiving end via a computer network. The learning end has radio listening facility as well as a computer screen to receive the textual data. Since both audio and text are broadcast simultaneously, the learner at the receiving end gets high quality and low cost teaching. An experiment on the use of radio-text at Yashwant Rao Chavan Maharashtra Open University, Nasik, India resulted in the satisfaction of more than 80 percent the learners. It also used for peer group discussion at the receiving end after the broadcast, which indicates radio-text could be used for varieties of objectives.

Women's Participation

Stereotyped portrayal of women in media messages is a universal axiom, though definitions of what constitutes a stereotype way vary across cultures. Likewise one can find similarities in feminist reactions towards advertise-ments across cultures and geographical boundaries. So much so that portrayal of women in media has become a global sensitivity. Furthermore, in the past decade media analysis has become an important agenda of action for many women activists groups and other organisations. Among young women (college going) there is a strong perception that obscene film songs lead to eve teasing and harassment. The positive sign in this situation is some increase in women's programmes of greater variety. But these kind of positive efforts have always remained limited. Hence we are one step forward but two steps backward.

There is manifold increase in vulgarity in the programmes and using women as commodity that cannot shape the attitude of gender equality. It is generally perceived that the main reason for exploitation of woman is her lack of control over these media. There is a constant demand to increase the representation by hiring and promoting more and more women at least in the government owned media organisations. However studies have indicated marginal or no improvement in this sector. It had been estimated that women formed 25 per cent in broadcasting in India in 1979.

A need to increase women's participation was felt by all the concerned hence greater participation in the future was expected. Especially when new developments had taken place like the development of the television. Instead the percentage of women in television centres was found lower than in 'broadcasting' in 1979. Among full time permanent employees 84-88 per cent are men and only 12-15 per cent are women in Doordarshan in 1994. However it seems that there is no substantial difference over the period of five years as the sample study states the range of 7% to 13% of women in administrative and 11% to 15% in production jobs in Doordarshan during 1989.

There is no simple explanation for the frequency of violent crimes against women, but it has been suggested that one contributing factor may be the way women are portrayed in the media. Women are often depicted as victims of violence or as sexual objects, and researchers have found that these media portrayals may influence how women are viewed and treated in society. Film, television, music, music videos and computer games have all been criticized for content considered demeaning to women, such as sexual objectification, depictions of violence against women, and the frequent association of violence with sexuality. Over 40 years of scientific investigation has led researchers to conclude that media violence significantly contributes to aggressive attitudes and behavior in society.

Mounting evidence suggests that negative perceptions of women in entertainment can affect women in real life. Research examining onscreen violence toward women finds that emotional desensitization can occur after viewing as few as two films with sexually degrading and violent themes. Studies also show that men who view a number of films in which women are portrayed in sexually degrading or violent situations become increasingly less disturbed by violence against women and less sympathetic toward female victims of violence. In addition, films initially found demeaning to women are judged to be less so after prolonged exposure. Some people target pornography as the medium most likely to depict women in an offensive manner.

Mainstream films and magazines are often more violent than pornography. In fact, the American public considers many movies demeaning to women; a survey found that 68% of the public believes sexual portrayals of women in American movies "often" amount to exploitation. Recent studies have found that college men exposed to just a few of these films tend to lack empathy towards female victims of rape, believing she "deserved what she got." In addition, these men often do not believe the rapist should be punished. On television, a disproportionate amount of violence is directed toward female victims. For every 10 male characters on primetime network TV who commit violence, 11 other male characters fall to violence, but for every 10 women who inflict violence, 16 women become victims.

Studies have shown that viewers who strongly associate with the victims (i.e., women) feel more susceptible to violence in the real world. More often than not, these viewers become the "real life" victims. Movies and television alone do not foster changes in attitude. Other media, including music and music videos, may also contribute to negative perceptions of women. Researchers have found an average of 18 instances of aggression each hour on Music Television (MTV), 35% of which depict sexual violence against women.

One study of 144 undergraduate males determined that after watching a significant amount of violent or demeaning music videos, desensitization occurs which may foster an antagonistic attitude toward women. Forty percent (40%) of the men in this study indicated some likelihood of committing rape if they could be assured of avoiding punishment. Studies show that the dominating theme of "love relationship" in songs has increasingly shifted to include explicit sexual references that are often demeaning to women. In particular, gangsta rap, a popular West Coast music style distinguished by lyrics that graphically describe scenes of gunplay, sex, drug use and violence, often depicts women negatively; their roles rarely extend beyond being kidnapped, held hostage, brutally gang raped at gunpoint, or murdered.

Studies have found that exposure to rap music does, in fact, "tend to lead to a higher degree of acceptance of the use of violence (including violence against women)." These types music videos communicate a dangerous message to both men and women - that the invasion of the female body is welcomed and desired, which may translate to rape in the real world. Video games can also portray violence against or degradation of women. In many, "women are usually cast as persons who are acted upon rather than as initiators of action; in extreme cases, they are depicted as victims." A study of 47 popular Nintendo games revealed that among 115 male and 9 female characters, 20 male and zero female characters had dominant roles.

Twenty-eight percent (28%) of the games in the study contained scenes depicting women as inferior and powerless. Some video games also perpetuate negative stereotypes about women and encourage players to participate in violence against them. In Duke Nukem, 3D players earn points by killing prostitutes. In addition to presenting women as sex objects, the game awards players for harassing women by throwing cash at them. One icon in computer games is the animated fantasy girl Lara Croft, who stars in Playstation's Tomb Raider. She is a female referred to as a "sex symbol with attitude." According to sociologists, games such as Tomb Raider encourage sexism and condition adolescents to view the world as they do the computer screen: with female sex symbols, female kidnapping, and female rescue and submission. In one study, up to one-third of parents were concerned about possible anti-social behavior (i.e., violence) influenced by these games.

As computers and Internet access become widespread, real-world crimes of harassment and stalking have moved on-line. It is estimated that one in twenty women will become targets of stalking behavior at least once during their lifetimes, and evidence suggests that the majority of cyberstalkers are men victimizing women. The Internet makes stalking, or "cyberstalking," much easier for the perpetrator than off-line stalking. The anonymity of e-mail and chat rooms cloak stalkers well, and stalkers can easily access private information about their victims via the Internet. Many on-line services and directories also enable individuals to obtain e-mail addresses, home addresses, and phone numbers without their intended victims knowing, since few people realize that their personal information is publicly listed online.

Cyberstalking is a relatively new phenomenon, but occurrences are becoming more frequent. In a national survey of college women during the 1996-97 academic year, 13% were stalked and 25% of those incidences reportedly involved cyberstalking. The Web Police, an international crime fighting agency, also estimated that about 30% of the 47,000 complaints it received in 1998 involved harassing or threatening e-mail, and seventeen states now have laws against on-line stalking and harassment. The Clinton administration has called for tougher laws against on-line stalking and encourages Internet companies to launch a web site to educate people about cyberstalking and how to protect themselves.

Influence on Children

Children internalize gender role stereotypes from books, songs, television, and the movies. Television, however, is perhaps the form of media most influential in shaping ideas of appropriate sex roles. Research on television viewing and the socialization of children indicates television has a great impact on the lives of children. Studies have shown preschoolers spend an average of nearly 30 hours a week watching television; it is suggested children spend more time watching television than they spend on anything else except sleeping. By the time children are sixteen years old, they have spent more time watching television than going to school. Children are exposed to about 20,000 advertisements a year.

By the time children graduate from high school, they have witnessed 13,000 violent deaths on television. Prosocial and antisocial behaviors are influenced by television. Also, television influences attitudes about race and gender. As children grow and develop, they are taking in information and acquiring knowledge at a rapid pace. As children develop their cognitive abilities, they assimilate new information into their existing knowledge base and adjust to the new information by accommodating it to what they already know. Children's ideas about how the world works come from the experiences they have and the attitudes and behaviors they see around them.

The young child who comes to understand women are nurses and men are doctors may have come to the realization because the first doctor he or she saw was a man, and he was assisted by a female nurse. This man as doctor, woman as nurse idea may have reinforced by parents reading books; conversations with friends and television may reinforce also. If the child frequently is faced with gender biases and gender stereotypes, this knowledge will be incorporated and influence perceptions regarding men and women. Keeping in mind young children with developing minds watch many hours of television, and recalling television reinforces gender stereotypes, it is not surprising children come away from this television experience with firmly held beliefs. Frequently these beliefs are stereotyped with regard to gender.

Of the various factors which help shape gender-typed behaviors, role models and imitation are extremely influential. Children are exposed to models throughout their environment, including those on television. Research suggests children who view violent programming on television will behave more aggressively with peers. It is also true children who view prosocial behaviors on television are likely to exhibit those types of behaviors themselves. Young children will imitate and repeat behaviors they see on television. Because children are influenced by gender stereotyped role models they see on television, they will also exhibit gender biased behaviors and develop gender biased attitudes that they see modeled on television.

Positive developmental outcomes for young children during their growing-up years include developing autonomy, initiative, and a sense of industriousness. Children who witness female characters on television programs who are passive, indecisive, and subordinate to men come to understand this is the appropriate way for females to behave. It is less likely for female children to develop autonomy, initiative and industriousness when they rarely see it modeled in those around them. Similarly, because male characters on television programs are more likely to be shown in leadership roles and exhibit assertive, decisive behavior, children learn this is the appropriate way for males to behave.

While some children's programming has come under attack for being violent, irrelevant, or sexist, other programs for children, such as Sesame Street, are regularly lauded for attempting to meet the developmental needsof children. Sexism, however, can be found even among the Muppets, who all have male names or male voices. A study of Saturday morning cartoons found females were pictured less often than males, were less active than males, played fewer roles than males, played fewer lead roles than males, and worked primarily in the home. Although these findings were obtained two decades ago, there has been no improvement. Females are not more fairly represented in children's programming. Recent studies of Saturday morning programs for children demonstrated males are featured in dominant roles, while females are shown in peripheral roles.

Children's programs on the Public Broadcasting System have consistently shown fewer females than males. Further, television programs evidence a greater range of occupations for males than females. This discrepancy in occupations between males and females is shown on music television, where it was found that more than nine out of ten occupational roles classified as stereotypically male (e.g., physician, mechanic, firefighter) were played by male actors. It has been suggested the preferences of boys are given precedence over those of girls because boys represent 53% of the Saturday viewing audience. Those who make decisions regarding children's programming have determined action and violence should dominate children's television.

Gender stereotypes occur with frequency on daytime soap operas; women are often shown as hopeless individuals, unable to solve problems without assistance. Both males and females are shown in gender stereotypic roles on many music television programs. Children frequently watch these programs after school, and receive reinforcement for the notion women are subordinate, passive, and indecisive. About two-thirds of characters in television programs are male. From the 1950s through the 1990s, this figure has remained stable.

There is more interaction shown with men (with both men and women) than there is with women. Further, interactions between men and women frequently indicate women are defined by their relationships with men. Television often does not reflect reality when it deals with the occupations of men and women. For example, programs depict 75% of women as being in the labor force, compared with the truer figure of about 56%. The primary job setting for most women on television is as a professional. Most women in real life, however, are in low paying, low status jobs.

Lessthan 10% of women in the United States make more than $50,000 a year. Most females on nighttime television are young, attractive, thin, and ornamental. Most female characters are either under 35 or over 50. Middle-aged women are rare. Females are consistently placed in situations where looks count more than brains, and helpless and incompetent behaviors are expected. Men are twice as likely as women to be shown as competent and able to solve problems. Gender stereotypes abound on television, with women being depicted as sex objects more frequently than men, and men portrayed as inept when handling children's needs.

On music television, a popular program choice among young viewers, females are often shown in degrading positions. Music videos frequently show women as sex objects. Females are also shown as trying to gain the attention of a male who ignores them. Rap music videos are also popular with young television viewers. Frequently women are portrayed as objects of lust. Women are four times more likely than men to be provocatively dressed; while men are almost always fully clothed. While early television commercials were criticized for being overwhelmingly biased in favor of males, a study of commercials broadcast between 1971 and 1985 indicated improvement regarding numbers of male and female main characters.

However, even though there is currently more equity in the number of men and women appearing in commercials, women are most often shown in the role of wife and mother, or in demonstrating products for the home. Another aspect of television advertising which is overwhelmingly a masculine province is voiceovers and narration, in which 83-90% of the voices are male. In commercials for children's programs, boys are shown more frequently and in active roles; girls' behavior is much more likely to be passive. Advertisers indicate male models generate more product sales to children of both sexes than female models. It has also been suggested girls watch male-dominated programs and commercials because there are few other options. Girls will become loyal to programming that is more gender fair. Interestingly, children without television have been shown to be less stereotyped in their gender role attitudes. Children who view programs with non-traditional gender roles tend to have non-traditional gender role perceptions. Because children model behavior they see on television, they are likely to perpetuate gender stereotypes they view.

Influence on Youth

The media executives are quick to defend their role in youth violence and bullying while selling millions of dollars in add space focused on youth. Lets take a closer look at the reality of this issue. TV producers, network executives, motion picture companies and others in the media world downplay and deny any impact of their programs on the attitudes and actions of youth. Meanwhile they continue to spend millions on special effects and marketing geared to increase appeal to youth markets. While corporations spend millions on market research and advertising to create products and campaigns targeted at a youth demographic, they still deny their ability to influence youth attitudes and culture.

Clothing companies are spending millions to get young good-looking individuals to make plain and boring clothes look appealing to youth. Youth respond to visual advertising more than other forms. This is due to the fact that youth want to visualize them selves using the product or service. An example of this would be simply as follows. Even adults are manipulated by these practices. For example, Roots comes out with a new hat. You hear an ad for this hat on the radio. You may be curious but you cannot visualize the actual style or yourself wearing this item. Next you see the ad in a newspaper. Now you can visualize the product but it is only a photo. Now you see a television commercial. The persons in the commercial are snowboarding and having fun. A song is playing in the ad that catches your ear. Now you subconsciously associate the product with fun, excitement and style.

Now you want to go and purchase that hat. This is a plain and straight example of how the media in it's simplest for influences youth culture. Now if you consider how often youth are subjected to the idea that you need to look perfect, be thin, use violence and smoke cannabis etc. it is a powerful and effective influence or it would not be such big business. If they took more responsibility in the attitudes they are creating they are scared that they would not make the revenues that they currently enjoy. This has an effect on society on a whole because of the younger kids looking up to the older youth for guidance. They want to mimic the older youth as they see as "cool". Adults have a desire to look and feel younger and therefore they tend to follow youth trends in order to facilitate this behaviour. Thus the media has a large influence on society as a whole. They effectively manipulate and create false perception to further their own financial objectives.

The mass media affects the lives of our young by acting as a substitute for a number of institutions and social contacts, by providing information and entertainment, by creating and mediating art, etc. In this way, it fulfills a variety of functions in human life. The time spent in front of the television screen is usually at the expense of leisure: there is less time for games, amusement and rest. Most often children look upon television as a certain kind of socially beneficial instrument, an open door into the world of the imagination. Attracted by what is happening on the screen, children not only imitate what they see but directly identify themselves with different characters. The Surgeon General also states that Americans have been concerned about the prevalence of violence in the media and its potential harm to children and adolescents for at least forty years. During this period, new media emerged, such as video games, cable television, music videos, and the Internet.

Current psychological theory suggests that the interactive nature of many of these new media may affect children's behavior more powerfully than they have thought in the past. As they continue to gain popularity, these media, along with television, prompt public concern and research attention. Another large societal concern on our young generation inflicted by the media, is body image. External forces can influence body image positively or negatively. For one, societal and cultural norms and mass media marketing impact our concepts of beauty. In the mass media, the images of standardized beauty fill magazines and newspapers, beam from our televisions and entertain us at the movies. Even in advertising, the mass media plays upon accepted cultural values of thinness and fitness for commercial gain. Young adults are presented with a narrowly defined standard of attractiveness, an ideal that carries unrealistic physical expectations.

Sometimes, men or women will result to drastic measures to fit the image they want to be, or the image that they feel society will accept them. In doing so, disorders can develop, such as Anorexia nervosa and Bulimia nervosa. Anorexia nervosa generally starts between 12-18 years of age, and is characterized by restrictive food intake, weight loss and excessive exercise. One half to one percent of adolescent girls develops anorexia. Another eating disorder that is common is Bulimia nervosa, which is the binge/ purge syndrome. It typically develops between sixteen to twenty years of age. Approximately three percent of teenage girls develop bulimia. These percentages do not include all those who have these disorders, only those that have reported their' eating disorders.

Many people can hide their disorder very well, and can result in death. The mass media can affect children's thinking and behaviors. For many young people, the world on the television screen is a more frequent topic of conversation than events and unpleasant moments in school or at work, than the opposite sex, and what friends are doing, etc. Compared with television, the other mass communication media form a substantially smaller part of the daily topics of conversation. Also, television watchers can be influenced positively or negatively by what they see on the screen and can go out into the world, imitating these acts.

Also, the media portrays an unrealistic body image for adolescents and all of society. This struggle to be accepted by society can lead to feelings of depression, anger, and anxiety and even direct to eating disorders. Two common known eating disorders prevalent in society are Anorexia nervosa and Bulimia nervosa. Both disorders are common in society and can result in death if not treated. In closing, the media should be of great concern to our society. Delivering wrong messages and unrealistic images by the media can only cause problems and trouble for our youth. Although the sole purpose of the media is enjoyment for society, the public should be aware that it could sometimes cause negative effects on its viewers.

Media Violence

The effect of media violence on the human mind has been a subject of debate over decades. Newspaper headlines have linked bizarre crimes to specific examples of media coverage, and the protection of children from media violence crops up periodically as a media issue. Yet although the debate seems no closer to being resolved than it was back in the 1950s, there is a substantial body of research on the patterns of media violence and the possible effects of media violence on the consumer.

Structural violence (social injustice) is of only subordinate importance in entertainment broadcasts. Violence is presented almost exclusively in connection with individual fates, with no insight into possible socio-structural determinants of the violence. The most violent protagonists by far are unmarried men of middle age. Violence is shown as typically linked with the masculine role. As a rule, aggressive dynamic men aged 30 to 40 are surrounded by beautiful soft women aged 20 to 30. In TV entertainment an image of women is drawn that has predominated in European art since the Middle Ages; the woman is passive and seductive.

Typically violent acts occur in the TV broadcasts between protagonists who are strangers to each other, in speaking distance of one another. This depiction is most unrealistic as in most cases violence is the result of an interaction sequence between individuals who know each other, e.g. members of a family. The most frequently shown form of violence is that of a clearly dominant attacker who damages and/or overpowers another. Depiction of the violence itself is extremely unrealistic. Although an act of violence can cause death of the recipient, the suffering of the victim, blood and wounds are shown only rarely.

In the world of TV entertainment hardly a protagonist dies a natural death. The focus is on the performing of violence, i.e. on "action". As a rule the victim is presented only briefly. Violence is shown as an efficient instrument for attaining goals or solving conflicts, When a negative main protagonist who uses violence is punished, this mostly happens at the end of a film plot, after violent behaviour was previously successful in many individual sequences. Violence is not only used by "negative" protagonists but also just as often by representatives of law and order (police or private detectives) to help uphold the law. Whoever becomes violent because of loyalty to the law as a rule has nothing to fear.

Witnesses to violent events as a rule do not try to mediate or help but usually remain passive. In summary, TV violence is linked to the masculine role and is (carried out) between strangers. Although violence can be fatal for the recipient, it is very rarely painful. Television offers behaviour models demonstrating how with illegitimate means (violence) aims recognised as legitimate (prosperity, power, prestige, justice) are achieved. There are, of course, detractors from the notion that media violence causes harm to viewers and readers. A major criticism of the "media effects" theory is that it assumes that readers and audiences are passive sponges, unable to sift what is within a media genre from what is real life.

Active audiences, this theory maintains, are trained through a lifetime of viewing to tell screen violence from real violence, to enjoy the first as a form of entertainment but to naturally eschew the second. Traditional definitions of "violence" have also been criticised. According to Martin Barker the expression "media violence" has to be one of the most ill-informed of all time. "It is supposed to encompass everything from cartoons (ten-ton blocks dropped on Tom's head by Jerry, children's action adventure films (the dinosaurs of Jurassic Park...) news footage from Rwanda and Bosnia; documentary footage showing the police attacking Rodney King in Los Angeles; horror films from Hammer; the range from Clint Eastwood as the voiceless hard man of Dirty Harry to Arnie as the violent humorist of almost any of his films, etc, etc. No single ground has ever been given for us to suppose that such a list has any single property in common...it is a useless conflation of wholly different things."

Yet another exception generally taken is that research methods are crude and you cannot measure human reaction the way you observe Pavlovian dogs. But crude or not, a substantial body of research does exist to show that media violence has definite effects on consumers. Edward Donnerstein found that the level of aggression of male subjects toward females increased after they had been exposed to violent pornography in which a female rape victim was portrayed as becoming aroused by the end of the movie. (Aggression was measured by the intensity of electric shock that subjects were willing to administer.) Violent films that were non-pornographic (depicting, for example, a man hitting a woman) also increased subjects' levels of aggression toward hitting women, but not to the same extent as violent pornographic films.

Other studies have found that prolonged exposure to filmed violence desensitizes subjects. In one particular study, subjects were exposed to five consecutive days of viewing violent films. Subjects' perceptions of the violence portrayed in the films also changed over the five days. The films were perceived to be significantly less violent by the last day of viewing. Ratings of how degrading the film was to women and of its offensiveness were also significantly lower by the last day. There is a tendency for such desensitisation to "spill over" into subjects' judgements of a female victim in another context. Men who were exposed to the large doses of filmed violence against women judged the victim of a violent assault and rape to be significantly less injured and evaluated her as generally less worthy tan the control group of subjects who saw no films.

Subjects who rated the material as less offensive or violent and more enjoyable by the last day of viewing were much more likely to judge the victim as more responsible. These findings add strength to the mounting evidence that sustained exposure to filmed violence may lower sensitivity to victims of violence in other contexts." If such findings are applied to the news coverage of violence against women, it becomes clear that it is the media's responsibility not to identify, blame or judge female rape victims and not to make judgements of domestic abuse survivors. It also becomes important not to eroticise violence.

Ethnic identity is defined to broadly include religious, linguistic, ethnic, communal, caste and other historical and cultural definitions that provide a deep rooted social identity to a community and help to separate it from other communities living in India. India is not only a very big and populous country; it is also a very diverse country. There are about 16 main languages and a large number of dialects. Hindus form over 80 per cent of the population. But there is a fair number of several other religions like Muslims (about 12 per cent), Christians (about 4 per cent), Sikhs, Buddhists and Jains being the other religions though on a smaller extent. There is a prevalence of hierarchical caste system within the Hindus. In addition, there is enormous geographical diversity with climates varying from extremely hot to extremely cold, variation in food habits, cultural forms of art and performance, social practices, etc.

There is also diversity in terms of the levels of developments in the country. On the one hand India has the third largest scientific manpower in the world and on the other nearly 48 per cent of the population is illiterate. There are research and academic institutes of a very high order and at the same time there are several villages deprived of the basic amenities like elementary schools, primary health centres, clean drinking water, etc. In spite of all these differences and diversity, there is a common element of "Indianness" binding the country together. This common binding can only be described as "Indianness" because it rises beyond the boundaries of religious, languages, castes, geographical or even political barriers. It may be composed of all these elements but is not circumscribed by it. The end product is clearly more than the mere sum total of different elements. The oft-mentioned Indian unity in diversity is not a mere slogan or cliché, because India has a very long history of harmonious co-existence between different ethnic groups.

It is true that there are occasional conflicts, sometimes very virulent and long persisting, but by and large, the society has displayed remarkably harmonious relations. In a sense there is a constant interplay between assertion of individual or group identity and being part of the national mainstream or even belonging in some way to the international community in today's global village. This interplay between assertion of individual identity and being part of a mainstream may lead to stress or conflicts. But they are not necessarily contradictory or conflicting.

Every individual belongs to a small ethnic group - linguistic, regional, religious, etc. and at the same time is a citizen of the country, is a member of international group and thus wears multiple roles but they are not necessarily conflicting. Another important feature of the Indian nation is that it is a democracy. In spite of several pulls, pressures, stresses and occasional distortions in its functioning, it has remained an active and a vibrant democracy for more than 50 years. The country has endowed itself with a very liberal constitution where equality under the law and the freedom to practice one's religion has been guaranteed.

Freedom of expression and the rule of law have been ensured in the constitution. While certain amount of conservatism may be a part of the Indian ethos - as is likely to be the case with any ancient civilisation - it has always been receptive to new ideas and new technologies. The role of the media has to be understood in this overall socio, cultural, political context. The Indian media scene is also extremely diverse. India is the producer of largest number of feature films in the world, publishes a very large number of newspapers and magazines in different languages (300 English dailies and 3936 regional language dailies), the reach of the electronic media of radio and television has been expanding at a very rapid rate (57.7million TV households in 1996 and an estimated 111 million radio sets). The Indian television landscape shows that the penetration of the foreign satellite channels is expanding very fast (with 14.2 million Satellite households having access to 4 English, 22 Indian language and 5 channels in both languages).

At the same time the reach and popularity of the national television system has continued to hold sway. There are several people who read foreign magazines but also read Indian magazines. Thus the Indian audience is open to both domestic and international media consumption. It is inherent to any medium that it plays a very significant dual role. The media have to reflect the reality as well as shape and change it. It cannot go overboard in attempting to shape the reality for that will distance it from the social and cultural ethos with the eternal danger of being rejected nor can it be a passive spectator and merely reflect or reinforce the realities.

The media have to contribute to the individual, local, regional, national and international needs. It has to actively participate in assertion of the ethnic identities and ethnic demands and also being participatory and non-parochial. There has to be a fine balance between the group rights and the larger social good. In reality which media play what type of a role has been a question bothering social scientists and communication researchers and people at large especially in today's context of the communication revolution.

5

Multicultural Media Monitoring

Racism never has been limited to extremist right-wing parties, and these parties or similar racist organizations are not the only and not the most important reason for concern. Rather, racist ideas that once were expressed only on the extreme Right have now affected mainstream parties. Immigration is severely being restricted in virtually all countries of the European Union and elsewhere in Western Europe, and the European Fortress is no longer merely a rhetorical scare-word, but begins to take an increasingly concrete form.

Besides these official political measures to "curb" the immigration of unwanted Others, each domain of European societies shows signs of deteriorating human rights. Attacks on immigrants have become so widespread and common, not only in Germany, that they are no longer even routinely covered in the media. More or less subtle discrimination and everyday racism in housing, employment, health care, legislation, and policing have become general practice.

As may be expected from mainstream institutions, the media are an inherent part of that problem. Especially the conservative and popular press indulges in sometimes blatant "foreigner-bashing" and the reproduction and affirmation of racist prejudices. Popular resentment against refugees and other immigrants and minorities is thus both legitimated and at the same time exacerbated. Politicians in turn respond to the popular resentment they have helped create through the media in the first place by ever tougher legislation against immigration.

Even the more liberal and quality press does not systematically and critically oppose the rising tide of racism. On the contrary, they have taken part in the well-known elite denial of racism, especially also by ignoring their own role in the elite management of 'race relations'.

In line with the prevalent no-nonsense policies that are leading to the gradual destruction of the welfare state, also these race relations policies have become harsher, and such policies are generally supported, or at least hardly criticized by the elite press. The forms this popular and elite press response to immigration and increasing multiculturalism has taken are among the following:

— Immigration is generally defined as a serious problem, as a threat or an invasion, and never as a welcome contribution to ethnic and cultural diversity, the economy and the demography of Western Europe.

— Refugees and other new immigrants are increasingly defined, also in the press, as impostors, scroungers or otherwise defined as negative; and increasing limitations of their rights welcomed, or hardly criticized.

— Similarly, in all societal domains, the presence of new immigrants or resident minorities, continues to be portrayed in similarly negative terms, that is as a problem, if not as a threat to the Nation.

— In the news negative other-presentation combined with self-serving positive self-presentation is as routine as in other types of elite discourse. Thus, crime reporting still associates minorities with specific forms of 'ethnic' crime, such as aggression, mugging, rioting, theft, prostitution and especially drugs.

— In the same perspective, prevalent everyday racism is ignored or denied, and seldom defined as Our problem. Only racist violence and aggression or blatant forms of discrimination are criticized. Everyday discrimination in many domains of society is hardly newsworthy.

— The prevailing discrimination by employers, which is among the main causes of high minority employment, is seldom critically analyzed. Programs of affirmative action, if any, are generally rejected both by employers and politicians, as well as by the media and other elite institutions, and often presented as "unfair competition" or as "favoring foreigners"; they may exacerbate popular resentment-again, a form of resentment they have helped define and create in the first place.

— Topics that are especially relevant for minorities are virtually excluded, so that the top five topics associated with minorities is in fact a standard list of stereotypes rather than an account of the multiple newsworthy events, domains and actions in which minorities are involved.

— Minority organizations, leaders and spokespersons have less access to the media than their 'white' mainstream counterparts, even in news that directly concerns them, and about which they may be seen as experts. They are less quoted, and less credibly quoted, than mainstream news actors and organizations.

— The increasing number of competent minority journalists face systematic forms of discrimination in hiring, and if they are hired at all, in promotion. Virtually no European newspaper has minority editors or in other prominent positions.

— Journalists generally resent even voluntary codes for adequate reporting on 'race', and see such codes as a limitation of the freedom of the press.

— There is no special training for young journalists in the balanced coverage of multi-cultural society.

In sum the role of the media in the increasingly multi-cultural and multi-ethnic societies of the Europe is crucial. Whereas many, if not most, native citizens in most countries have little or no daily interaction with immigrants, information about immigration as well as ethnic groups, events and relations is largely based on information from the mass media.

Research in several countries has repeatedly shown that although few major media, and especially television and the quality press, are explicitly and blatantly racist, few media play a positive role in the active promotion of a just and peaceful multicultural society. Minority journalists are as discriminated against as workers in any other social domain. Seldom stereotypical, and rather exclusively focuses on negative events and situations, and attributes associated with, if not explicitly blamed on ethnic minorities, immigrants or refugees. On the other hand, similarly detailed negative and critical accounts of everyday discrimination and racism by members of the majority, and especially among the elites, are lacking.

News gathering, story assignment, topics, quotation, and style are thus systematically stacked against the Others. It is not surprising, in light of this incontrovertible scholarly evidence, that-exacerbated by social and economic problems-widespread resentment against immigrants and minorities are stimulated and confirmed by such media practices.

Therefore, as is the case for all domains, sectors and institutions of all European countries, it is imperative that such media practices be monitored on a regular basis, and various measures be taken to improve them within the overall goal of shaping a viable, humane and peaceful multicultural Europe.

Given the essential freedom of the press, such an aim can obviously only be reached if journalists themselves identify with such multicultural aims and become both personally and institutionally involved in the creation of truly multicultural media. However, other institutions and organizations are also needed to cooperate in the realization of this aim.

Thus, universities or professional schools are involved in the education of journalists as well as in research on the coverage of ethnic affairs in the media. And yet, the main responsibility lies with the media themselves, and a media monitoring project can be successful and effective only when it is able to persuade journalists to change their practices.

By 'media monitoring' we shall here understand a series of observational, analytical, evaluative and critical activities by independent (non-media) organizations focussing on the practices and the products of mass media and media workers. Such a critical evaluation of media performance presupposes a set of criteria and values and aims at an improvement of media practices and products in light of fairly generally accepted social, cultural and political conceptions about the role of the media in society.

Hence, media monitoring is not a form of control, let alone a limitation of the freedom of the press. Its aim is not to impose or advocate prohibitions, but to persuade media workers to adopt or enact recognized professional standards of quality, balance, fairness and social responsibility.

In the context described above of growing intolerance, xenophobia and racism in Europe, such standards have become especially important if the media are to play a positive role in the development of egalitarian multicultural societies in which the human rights of immigrants and minorities are respected.

Media monitoring should be carried out by people or groups who understand media practices, products and organization, or who are specialized in a relevant dimension of media performance or its role in society. That is, media monitoring may variously focus on the following aspects of the media:

- schooling of journalists and other media workers
- hiring and promotion of media workers, also from minority groups
- training on the job
- the general 'management of diversity' in the media organization
- the development and evaluation of non-racist and multicultural policies
- new and refresher courses on multicultural reporting
- relations with other organizations and institutions, e.g., those of politics
- news gathering routines
- the use of, or interaction with sources
- using press releases or other documents
- participating in press conferences
- interviewing news sources and guests at programs
- writing news, editorials and background articles
- dealing with readers
- the various products of media workers: news, articles, documentaries, film, advertisements, shows, etc.

Despite this variety of dimensions of the media involved in media monitoring, many of the monitoring activities focus on the evaluation of the actual 'products' of the media: news and background articles in the press, and various programs on television. However, if critical analysis of such products concludes that such products are not up to standards, several other dimensions of the organization of media institutions may be considered, viz., as a mode of explanation or in view of recommending improvements.

Thus, unbalanced or biased topic choice in reporting about ethnic affairs may be attributed to inadequate education, the absence of a code or policy for such reporting, failing editorial control, and/or to the lack of minority reporters or editors in the newsroom. Critical analysis and evaluation is merely one side of media monitoring.

Even more important are the establishment of good relationships with the media, the constructive and persuasive formulation of alternatives and improvements, involving management, editors as well as reporters and other media workers, and in general all activities that aim at an effective improvement of media performance according to the criteria set by generally accepted and respected social and media values. At this point, strategies need to be worked out and links with other organizations may need to be made. Further activities may include documentation, training and lectures, and in some cases also litigation.

Hence, it is here proposed to set up, fund and support a restricted, flexible and cost-effective system of monitoring working groups. These small working groups would be responsible for monitoring a highly selective number of influential media, such as major national newspapers and popular TV programs. Their analyses would focus primarily on those properties of media products and other activities that are especially relevant for the role of the media in a multicultural society. Initial, preparatory, work of such bureaus should consist of getting some schooling in media monitoring and the analysis of media and racism, reading relevant literature on the media in multicultural societies, developing evaluation criteria, contacting similar groups abroad, and so on.

In a next phase, actual monitoring will begin by identifying which newspapers, programs or networks will be covered, registered, coded, documented, analyzed and/or evaluated. Contacts will be established with journalists or other workers related to these media or programs, so as to guarantee in an early stage that future cooperation with these will be possible. The main phase of monitoring is the routine registration, documentation and analysis of media content and practices. Critical evaluation, based on relevant criteria is the main immediate goal of such monitoring.

However, the ultimate goal is change: To persuade mediamakers to adapt their work to the criteria of professional quality, fairness, and social responsibility within the broader framework of the role of the media in society. That is, in the crucial final phase of monitoring, regular interaction with mediamakers will be necessary to discuss the implications of critical evaluation and recommendations. Strategies may be jointly developed to improve media output, such as improving journalism education, training on the job, seminars, enhanced editorial control, and closer involvement of readers or social organizations.

6

Media Flow and World Wide Web

Typically defined as a network of networks, the Internet is also a range of computer applications which structure and enable communication in a variety of ways. E-mail is typically a private one-to-one form of computer-mediated communication. "Chat" environments are often one-to-one, although not always private and can sometimes more closely resemble small group communication. As a communication medium then, the Internet can be viewed as a mixture of social practices which take place over distributed computer networks.

Recently, the social practices enabled by the World Wide Web (WWW) have come to represent the future direction of Internet communications. The WWW, first proposed in 1989, has expanded beyond its original aims of promoting collaboration amongst scientists to serving as the public face of the Internet for its widespread diffusion in industrialised countries. In net jargon, it is the definitive "killer app." An application whose development and functional capabilities have become a new paradigm for exchanging information and communicating via the Internet.

The increasing prominence of the WWW has led to many changes in use of the Internet. Most notably amongst them has been the emergence of a critical mass of users which has not only radically re-oriented the priorities of a pre-existing online services industry, but also the viability of using the medium in increasingly commercial ways. The 1993 release of the first graphical Web browser, MOSAIC, is perhaps the single most profound event in the development of computer-mediated communication.

The growth of Internet use has been phenomenal during this period, signaling a boom for other industries as well. Computer sales, telecommunications traffic and the emergence of Internet Service Providers, amongst others, are a testimony to the increasing value of computer-mediated communication.

As the Internet and the WWW have come to stand for a diverse range of social practices it is difficult to predict future developments. The flexible nature of the medium coupled with the relative volatility of industries which support its development, makes it very difficult to foreshadow the future. For example, an increase in the cost of a local telephone call, or the introduction of timed local calls, could radically restructure use of the Internet by increasing the importance of time, bandwidth and traffic volume as a concern for Internet users. This simple change in the telecommunications industry could squelch the public's interest in home-based Internet communications and, by restricting the online services industry's ability to generate revenue, potentially decrease the attractiveness of new generations of multimedia computers, amongst other things.

The Internet as it is realised today rests upon a precarious mutual interdependence between high-tech industries. However, as the Internet and, more specifically, the World Wide Web become increasingly integral to the publicity, sales, and service delivery aspirations for the corporate sector, the number of stakeholders participating in its development increases.

As the WWW becomes increasingly commercial in character, the communication it enables is increasingly similar to the type of communication enabled by the development and institutionalisation of previous media technologies. As a result, currently witnessing the emergence of traditional broadcasting industry configurations between the broader online industry, its texts and audiences. These trends represent a stark contrast between current uses of the Internet and the rhetoric which has surrounded it throughout much of its development.

The historical development of the Internet has been well documented. It is not my intention to trace that trajectory, again, here. However it is important to point out that recent trends in computer-mediated communication, such as the impact of the World Wide Web on the growth of Internet usage and its increasing commercial character, strike a marked difference from its previous incarnation as a government supported infrastructure used by researchers and academics. This difference is not only apparent in terms of content but also in the way the medium is used.

These changes force one to take stock of previous claims surrounding the social, political and cultural importance of the Internet and dissect the discourses which have constituted the environment of ideas in which actual policy and industry decisions regarding its future are made. Traditionally, these discourses have based our understanding of computer-mediated environments on the decentralised and interactive nature of computing technology. From this emanates the tendency to contrast computer-mediated communication with the form of communication associated with the centralised institutions of broadcasting and the seemingly passive reception of content it promotes.

The two discourses implicated here are, firstly, those which articulate the connection between use of the Internet and public participation in civic affairs, as well as, those which stress a new form of textuality emanating from the use of hypertext. The first discourse addresses the potential for Internet communication to form a new benchmark for citizen access to information and power. The second discourse addresses the cultural impacts of the non-linear, or multisequential, nature of hypertext and calls into question our traditional assumptions regarding the heretofore passive role ascribed to "readers" in the production of meaning and therefore their susceptibility to "preferred meanings" and ideological encoding.

This type of thinking harks back to previous manifestations of the Internet as a public infrastructure. A time when the Internet was firmly rooted in the government and academic research labs of the 1980s. Other scholars have pointed to the degree to which traditional power structures, such as those based on gender and race, are replicated via the Internet despite the absence of a physical cues in text-based communication.

Indeed the very conceptualisation of democratic communication as being based on the clash of views, or consensus achieved through adversarial argumentation, as represented in the self-regulating nature of some Internet communities, does not reflect a healthy diversity of approaches to realising this concept. In other words, the prominence of this view in the rhetoric which surrounds the Internet is itself reflective of traditional western male hegemony with regard to constituting what counts as "rational" public life.

While the Internet is often used as a forum for political participation and hypertext does indeed represent more scope for the reader to affect the unfolding of a "text," the understanding of future developments in computer-mediated communication must be grounded in the analysis of actual social contexts in which the technology is used.

Various social contexts make use of the Internet differently. For some, Web publishing is a chance to add to the diversity of information available throughout the world and generate networks of contacts independent of geographical space. For others, it is another publishing venue from which to generate wealth. The WWW can accommodate both uses of the technology. As such, academic approaches to the Internet must be flexible enough to adapt to changing uses of the technology and be capable of addressing the broad range of applications which make up Internet use.

There has always been ambiguity regarding how to conceptualise Internet communications vis a vis traditional media forms. Is the communication enabled by the Internet a form of publishing? Is it private communication - like traditional, or "snail," mail? The confusion is heightened by the many software applications that can realise the communications potential of the Internet differently. At the end of the day, the Internet is series of telecommunications links using the TCP/IP suite of protocols, amongst a few others, to exchange information. Some argued, the Internet is an abstract transactional space. The software, hardware and technical standards which realize this space, encode its functionality and ultimately shapes and constrains the behaviors enabled via the medium.

World Wide Web as a Cultural Form

The Internet, as a packet switched data network, is often cast as a vast decentralised space with no center or hierarchy. As a result, understanding of the social, political and cultural implications of the Internet are based on a contrast with the centralised, and often tightly controlled, broadcast media. This contrast promotes speculation over the democratic impact of the Internet as potentially improving the overall health, diversity and participation in society's communications systems. While the lack of a central core of the Internet is true from the perspective of the network, its actual use and implementation can realise different results.

Technology and Cultural Form, William argued that to really understand the uniqueness of television as a communications technology one needs to analyse not only its content, but also the way television presents its content. Concepts like genre, borrowed from the analysis of film and literature, are able to deal with audiovisual content, but not the actual way that content is delivered via television. The concept of flow captures all the "messiness" of television as a cultural form and as it is integrated into a set of practices known as broadcasting.

In all developed broadcasting systems the characteristic organisation, and therefore the characteristic experience, is one of sequence or flow. This phenomenon, of planned flow, is then perhaps the defining characteristic of broadcasting, simultaneously as a technology and as a cultural form.

Williams was pointing to the fact that all forms of media were stand alone entities or events. Whereas with television, we are actually presented with various sequences of content with each channel presenting its own alternative version as a broadcasting strategy. Williams' concept of flow in television applies to interaction on the WWW as well. Rather than merely visiting a set of discrete content repositories, "browsing" the Web is actually more like constructing a "flow" from link to link and, most probably, site to site.

Of course, the interactive nature of Web environments gives the user more control over the flow than is the case in traditional broadcast media. On commercial television the flow is seemingly dominated by programming strategies aimed at holding an audience over an evenings' viewing as well as clustering specific demographic groups around specific times for the benefit of advertisers. The concept of genre is a key factor in allowing broadcasters to manage and plan a successful sequence or flow.

How then do Web designers manage and plan a successful flow? Observing recent trends in Web publishing reveals a number of strategies by which flow is managed, typically surrounding the strategic use of hyperlinks. The concept of genre also plays a key role in the enactment of flow via the WWW. However, wish to propose an alternative construction of genre to the one that is adapted from literature for the study of film and television: One that, rather, is based on the qualities of genre that are characterised by the knowledge are draw on in everyday interactions in real world social situations.

Indeed all social interaction, including computer-mediated communication, is generic to some extent. When communicate with others enact typical patterns of behaviour based on knowledge of social situations as well as social roles and types. These behaviours build into repertoires over time and become backdrop of cultural knowledge draw on in everyday life. When encounter others typically have some way of understanding who they are and what are both meant to be doing and saying.

Computer-mediated communication, including interaction over the WWW, works the same way, as users, over time, develop a sense of digital literacy by which they can interpret online encounters and behaviour. As such, based on generic expectations of digital events come to understand who people, or entities are, what they want, or are trying to accomplish.

One could argue that the very success of the graphical interface is the way it draws on taken for granted everyday knowledge through iconic and metaphoric representations of objects, events and types of space. Knowledge of genre is integral to ability to understand the WWW. As is the case with everyday social interaction, to be successful on the Web need to understand who are dealing with. As Web publishing becomes increasingly promotional in nature, need to look at how Web sites relate to the user as well as how they relate to the rest of the Web in order to meet with success. In the absence of a real world interlocutor, the textual cues through which dialogue partner is presented become vital to reconstructing their aims and purposes.

Genre and Relational Flow

The virtual spaces created by computer networks are only enabled through the concept of interface. At one point in time the interface to the world of cyberspace was distinctly unattractive and difficult to use.

Online services, such as text-based videotex systems, were greeted less than enthusiastically in their first commercial incarnations, the French Teletel system being the exception. Graphical Interfaces to the WWW have altered this situation dramatically and have laid the foundation for the emergence of a digital literacy which will shape future uses of the Internet. Interfaces are semiotic resources which construct or play on situation types. Situation types develop characteristic ways of conveying experience and encoding relationships which become a cultural resource that is known and made use of by participants.

The encoding of relational communication markers in the interface of automatic banking machines most likely promoted their use. Ironically, when compared to actual encounters with tellers in typical urban bank the interface is perhaps more polite and inviting than the grunts and monosyllabic patter that normally takes place. It is in this sense that the interface is a proxy for a real-world person.

On the Web, the participants would be the user and the Web site designer. However, it is important to note that while the relational proxy is encoded by the designer, it typically reflects the goals and aspirations of a third party organisation who has commissioned the use of Web technology. A user might be greeted with the friendliest of welcomes, but when something goes wrong they are greeted with "Error Type 1" or "Fatal Execution Error" - or worse, the computer might hang and not respond at all; the ultimate in rudeness. It is moments like these, points of Heideggerian breakdown in human-computer interaction, that the user is forced to question their taken-for-granted mode of operating and examine the cultural knowledge which has guided their behaviour.

By avoiding the temptation to draw upon face-to-face communication as a metaphor for interactions with computers, graphical browsers make better use of cultural knowledge of objects and events. Better in the sense that the experience offered by the WWW doesn't rely on a model for interaction that it can never carry through. Over time, experiences in these contexts for action contribute to the development of a digital literacy, which accumulates over time and becomes crucial to Web browsing.

However, resisting the temptation to model face-to-face interaction does not completely remove a relational element from interactions on the Web. Instead, it becomes even more crucial to understand the contextual factors regarding the type of relationship being offered, or realised, the more implicit it becomes. Knowledge of genre needs to move beyond equating the term with "types of content," to addressing the relational aspect of computer interaction and its connection to types of Web content.

As the WWW begins to generate some stability in the contexts for action it presents to users, come to understand what is being asked of us, who are dealing with and what might like to do. For example, knowledge regarding the structure and meaning of domain names can provide a Web browser with crucial contextual information.

Web sites from within the government top-level domain have different purposes and adopt different modes of address from those typical of the commercial domain. Likewise, understanding the relational tenor of a Web site, as it is encoded in the very structure of choices offered to the user, is undoubtedly important to the creation of a successful sequence, or flow, from both the user's and designer's perspective.

The recent proliferation of content on the WWW makes navigation more difficult and, as such, knowledge of how to design and realise a desirable relational flow increasingly becomes the primary focus of behaviour on the WWW. The future of the WWW is likely to continue to be preoccupied with the management of sequence and emerging trends point to the problems that arise in this area given the increasingly commercial nature of Web publishing. Prominent among these trends are the commodification of hyperlinks through the adoption of the Web advertising business model, the emergence of legal disputes over hypertext linking to other commercial Web sites, and the emergence of new client interfaces, known as "push media" which more closely resemble the techniques of broadcasting.

Constructing Relational Flow

Generating value from the WWW is increasingly dependent on being able to realise relationships which are commercial in orientation. As a result, Web design is increasingly oriented to the management and construction of flow. Like broadcasters, Web designers have traditionally developed strategies which focus on managing the potential sequence in which their content is revealed. Concerns over navigation encourage designers to encode an underlying structure to the site which can aid the user in conceptualising how the content is organised. The distributed nature of hypertext also forces one to consider the implications of how one Web site leads to another. Hyperlinking, or the practice of linking one's own material to others on the WWW, is indeed the very basis of what originally made the web attractive as a source of information.

Prior to the burgeoning popularity of the Internet, the Internet community was largely self regulating. Publishing on the Web came with certain non-binding responsibilities, such as considering how material added to, rather than merely duplicated, the available content on the Web. Conceptualising the WWW as an "infostructure" highlights the fact that the Web should first and foremost be an integrated resource for finding information and resources.

An infostructure is directly related to the realisation of collegial relationships and developing the Web into a mutually beneficial resource. The seamless integration of related but different material, achieved through hyperlinks between Web sites, adds value to the overall Web as an information repository.

However, one could argue that using the WWW to realise relationships which are primarily commercial in nature renders the practice of linking between sites problematic. One particular problem arises from the fact that linking to others on the WWW, rather than duplicating content and trying to provide it better than others, tends to lead people away from site. For Web sites dependent on advertising, the ethics of old are clearly not the most profitable way to generate value through Web publishing.

At one time the business model of online services was the dominant approach to generating revenue from the Web. Publications on the WWW sought to deliver content and interactivity which would attract significant subscription revenue. Today, the advertising-supported site is far more common. Advertising, typically in the form of clickable banners, is today the primary means of generating revenue through Web sites. Click-through rates, which represent the number of individuals one Web site delivers to another, can be measured to determine the success of a banner and, indirectly, the centrality of the advertising supported site within the potential flow of the WWW.

Advertising on the WWW reduces hyperlinks to a mere commodity. The goal of commercial Web publishing seeks to increase the centrality of one's Web site in order to extract the most value from links to advertisers. As a result, Web publishers increasingly share many of the same concerns as broadcasters, leading to a hierarchy of value among Web sites, based on types of content or services, or their ability to publicise the site. Web sites which are magnets to people browsing the Web are strategically placed to generate the most revenue from this type of business model.

Traditionally, these have been the large search engines, such as Digital Equipment Corporation's Altavista, Yahoo! and InfoSeek to name but a few. The Web outlets of the traditional broadcast media, such as CNN and Time's Pathfinder are also strategically placed in this hierarchy based on their ability to cross promote their sites through other media outlets. The use of advertising in this manner would suggest that the aims of Web site development are increasingly similar to the aims of broadcasters: Capture a large audience and hold them. In this way Web publishing is increasingly similar to broadcasting. In television broadcasting, genre is a way of constructing an audience for specific advertisers.

Indeed the archetype of TV genres, the soap opera, still bears this in its name. By trading on knowledge of Web genres and domain names, site designers have the same potential to manage and predict Web audience behavior. The more the potential flow becomes ingrained in the audience's understanding of how the technology actually works, the greater everyone's potential becomes to manage how a successful sequence might be enacted.

In some cases preferences are captured covertly, through the use of "cookies" which allow a Web server to keep track of visits to the site. Another example is the Firefly Web site, which allows users to register and indicate their preferences for popular entertainment products in order to locate an online chat partner with similar tastes. In general though, the main strategy involves not only commodifying the audience but also the flow which leads from the site. The fact that some outlets are more strategically placed than others to do this produces a hierarchy of value amongst Web sites.

In the process of being best placed to construct and distribute Web users as a commodity these sites are, in effect, best positioned to manage the concept of flow through the commodification of hyperlinks. Not all Web sites are created equal despite the decentralised nature of the Internet. The argument that all nodes on the network, from the perspective of the network, are equal, does not account for the fact that some will deliver content and services that make them more attractive.

Thus, the tendency in contemporary Web design is to, first, centralise the site in the overall flow, by providing an attractive service or content, and second, manage the audience's behaviour to either follow the link via the advertising banner or keep them viewing pages until they find a banner they would like to follow.

The tendency in Web publishing is to make every effort to centralise oneself within the constructed flow. CNET: The Computer Network, originally a media production arm of INTEL, established an advertiser supported network of sites dedicated to the distribution of shareware software and computer industry news in 1995. To accomplish this, CNET presents itself as a series of distinct Web sites specialising in specific information and services. Again, the implications here are the centralisation of one's content within the flow of users'/audiences' choices. Whereas we used to conceptualise the users' behaviour in terms of browsing, typically from site to site - CNET's approach allows the user to browse without ever having to leave its network of advertising supported sites.

The structure of CNET's domain names is the equivalent of a successful advertising slogan which places the telephone number of the proprietor within a clever jingle. By drawing on a simple easy to remember domain name CNET contributes to the spread of digital literacy while increasing the trademark value and notoriety of its Web sites.

In addition to the centralising tendencies of commodified hyperlinks, other issues have arisen which reveal the strategies of Web publishers in managing flow. In particular, disputes have arisen over the legality of linking to other commercial Web sites without permission or prior agreement as to the monetary value of such links.

Other cases of such disputes have also emerged on the WWW, although they typically involve smaller organisations linking to the content of larger more established media providers who generate their own copyrighted material. One such case, Washington Post vs. Total News Inc. involved the use of frames. The use of frames allows Web designers to firmly keep individuals browsing the Web within one Web site while also letting them roam the Web in another part of the screen. Clearly a desirable design goal given the centralising ambitions of contemporary Web design techniques. In the above case, the Washington Post's content was, in effect, presented out of context by its inclusion within the Total News' framed Web site. As a result, the Post's material appeared as though it was a natural part of the service provided by the Total News Web site.

The need to maintain and construct a valuable flow is already having an impact on the interface of the future. "Push media," so called because its content is delivered to the user rather than actively searched for, increasingly bypasses the WWW completely. Content is delivered directly to the user via e-mail or separate client software which automatically connects and downloads content directly from the company's server at the click of a mouse.

The Pointcast Inc.'s Pointcast Network and Berkely Systems Inc.'s AfterDark are two examples of companies' products with strategic alliances with respected content providers who make use of different client software to deliver information via the Internet. Users can download the content direct from the company's server after selecting what information they would like to receive. The content is then displayed, complete with advertising, via the client program or through a screen saver format. In some cases, the software comes complete with integrated Web client, providing an interactive display of the advertiser's site in combination with the pushed content.

In by-passing the WWW, push media typically provide a different means of realising the abstract transactional space of the Internet. Current Web browsers make the activity of searching for information explicit, drawing on traditional conceptualisation of the Internet as an active communications medium. Push media deliver content in a way more akin to traditional mass media. While this might be a welcome solution to information management in the face of so much abundance, it fundamentally alters traditional conceptualisation of how computer-mediated communication works.

Future interfaces are likely to reflect this shift away from the active browsing of links toward the transparent reception of content. Examples from the online multi-player gaming environment already abound with attractive graphical clients which cast the process of moving from server to server in a way which removes it from the metaphor of active information seeking. Time Warner's The Palace is a graphical chat environment which is distributed with the necessary server software to allow users to create their own graphical environments. As the quantity of information on the WWW becomes increasingly difficult to manage, push client software provides an attractive alternative to having to construct a desirable flow. From a publishing perspective, push media bypasses the need to compete within the hierarchy of values already established amongst Web sites.

The commodification of hyperlinks in advertising supported sites, legal disputes arising over the right to link to other sites on the WWW and the development of push media all point to the importance of maintaining a central position within the Web's overall flow. As a result, the strategies and design techniques represented on the Web today have more in common with the strategies and techniques of commercial broadcasters than previous conceptualisation of the Internet would have us believe.

The Internet is best understood as a relational medium. The diverse range of applications which enable communication via the Internet, at the most basic level, bring people into contact with one another. Rather than starting from more abstract potential outcomes of such contact, such as the Internet's impact on citizen participation or the textual qualities of hypertext, research on the future directions of the Internet should be grounded in the specific configurations of relationships realised through computer-mediated communication. By focusing on the actual social contexts in which the technology is applied, academic understanding of the Internet will be better placed to deal with potential paths of its future development.

7

International News Flows

In most major news channels across the regions of the world, there were the continual news-makers of the USA and Western Europe, the "hot spots" of Third World crisis and an comparatively invisible world of state socialism. The South did not learn much about other regions of the South. It made sense to claim that the world of the news was "known". International news flows were dominated by the "big four" Western news agencies, who through the numbers of international subscribers, amount of news material distributed daily, and number of journalists based around the world, were able to set a substantial part of the international news agenda.

There was an imbalance in news flow with the Third World receiving far more materials about the First World than vice-versa. Such evidence and arguments culminated in the demands for a New World Information and Communication Order. In the mid-1980s, the US, UK and Singapore withdrew from Unesco, one of the central fora for such debate; the NWICO spirit and debate continues in new gatherings such as the MacBride Roundtables.

Since 1989, the world has experienced significant political and technological changes which have again altered the environment of international news-gathering. Politically, the Soviet Union has splintered into independent republics, a world-shaking tremor which is in 1995 still producing numerous inter-national and inter-ethnic aftershocks in Bosnia, Azarbaijan/Armenia, Tadjikistan and latterly in Chechnya.

When the Second World fractured, the Third World became a numerical chimera. The construct of a Third World was anyway challenged by the rapid economic development of several countries, the NICs, most especially the little dragons of the ASEAN nations,which has often precipitated a new kind of "orientalism" in Western press discourse. While some analysts have spoken of Japan as occupying a "fourth world", such numerical labels seem to have decreasing utility in a globalised market environment with a number of key centres, shifting peripheries, and pockets of endemic poverty in the North.

Race and ethnicity seem to have been readopted as the new international codes of difference, both by discourses of 'otherness' but also through discourses of 'self'. The reawakening of religio-political identities, Islam in particular through the inspiration provided by the Iranian Revolution, is evident in many places, creating new-old global affinities of religious culture. The continuing difficulty of economic development in Africa, constrained further by World Bank and IMF-imposed conditions including structural adjustment programmes, have been evident in the crises in Somalia, Ethiopia and currently Rwanda. In a context of such flux and crisis, the questions as to what the international news agenda both is and should be have become urgent ones.

Technological Changes in International News Production

Global news-gathering has changed also, with the rapid distribution of live television news perhaps the key new ingredient in the global news enviroment. New technologies, based on a combination of geo-synchronous satellites, satphones and ENG cameras, have ushered in a new era of "live" coverage in which image and sound can be edited together in the field and transmitted together.

This gives the location-based journalist a potentially far more significant role in determining not only the news agenda but the orientation of the news story. Such technologies were suddenly evident in the coverage of the Second Gulf War in 1991, and the "live feed" element coupled with the control instruments of the news pool and Pentagon vetting of journalists precipitated the very real concerns about the accuracy and diversity of coverage. The same phenomenon has been apparent in the coverage of Somalia and Rwanda, Haiti and other recent "foreign" crises.

How does speed of coverage, "turbo news", affect the journalistic values and practices involved? What kind of news agenda evolves? Are there different ways of addressing a global news audience? What is the relation between the foreign-policy making apparatus and the news production apparatus, when journalists often have a better understanding of what is happening than do diplomats?

Not only have the technologies of news-gathering altered. There are also new corporate and regional players in international news provision. CNN is now a global player, although some argue that its reach is predominantly to elite audiences. BBC World Service Television is run as a commercial operation independent of the main public service structure of the domestic BBC and is actively developing international distribution channels, such as Orbit in to the Middle East.

Reuters has become one of the top five global media corporations with its own, diverse, modes of international news diffusion, including direct video feeds and on-line access to news texts. It mixes specialist, business, newsfeeds with broad-based international news provision —in the winter of 1995, it signed an agreement to provide news for

Murdoch's "Sky" — and has extensive holdings in some of the other major international news providers, such as Worldwide Television News; Indeed. there is such a pronounced tendency toward global concentration amongst the wholesalers of video news footage that this might well be even more marked than the "big four" domination of the older news wire services.

However new organizations such as European News Service (ENS) and Associated Press Television News (APTV) are poised to start global news operations. Also, the rise of CNN as a "global" news provider during the Gulf War caused considerable consternation amongst Arab states. Much of the very rapid development by Gulf states of satellite provision, telecommunications networks and varied forms of broadcast message delivery were precipitated by that crisis, both in an endeavour to provide the world with "local" news and to develop an Arab perspective on the news; Middle East Broadcasting based in London and UAE Radio and Television based in Dubai are both currently active in satellite-based delivery of international news.

The transnational satellite channels—CNN, BBC World Service Television, Sky News, the Japanese GNN and the Spanish ECO News - act as retailers but also produce their own news product, and provide a heavy news diet selected and packaged for "global" audiences.

Another significant tier of organizational actors, the regional news exchanges like Eurovision News Exchange, Asiavision, Arabvision, etc, take in mainly non-regional news feeds from the agencies and distribute to their respective national broadcasting organizations. In the main, the regional news exchanges include public service or government broadcasters, consider television news not a commodity but a public good, with cost-sharing of facilities supporting their non-profit exchange mechanisms.

There is strong competition across the three levels of players - the wholesalers, the transnational satellite channels and the regional news exchanges -that constitute the international news environment, with the latter facing particularly heavy pressure in the new deregulated, market-driven media environment. But the jockeying for new modes of distribution, the cost-sharing agreements and exchanges all mean that the neat distinction between these three "tiers" is itself beginning to blur.

Strong competition for global audiences, markets and influence exists amongst the Anglophone satellite news providers, who currently dominate the market. British televisual news production and exchange is world-renowned, of considerable status, maintains British political influence abroad and contributes to the British cultural export market.

CNN, the brash newcomer, specialises in live coverage with minimal contextualization, leaving the viewer to make sense of the story. BBC World Service Television is utilising indigenous journalists in many countries and expresses a desire to see local television production improve while CNN has World News Report, which broadcasts news stories produced abroad.

These two organizations can be seen as ideal-type models of British and American international news production and vie for influence and definitional power over the global news agenda. A comparison of the international news output of the two players should tell us something of the perceived priorities and policy-orientations of the international relations agenda of the new world order, perhaps mirroring the evident foreign policy differences between the USA and Britain/Europe as to appropriate policy, over Bosnia for instance.

However, at the same time as the global players consolidate, there has also been a growth of Southern international news gathering agencies attempting to provide something of a "contra-flow" to the major western agency news flow IPS has survived in Rome but appears to be pressured in the new political environment under Berlusconi, and may need to search for a new base of operations. Other agencies such as Gemini focus on news of the developing world, and there are also at least two services, Women's Feature Service and DepthNews, which provide international news and features with a specifically gendered perspective.

As much of contemporary theorizing suggests, there are powerful forces of globalization and homogenisation, but also significant forces of localization and heterogenization. Globalization includes the operation of financial markets, which create complex webs of economic integration and interdependence and allow for global movements of capital toward cheap labour, the growth of global media conglomerates which take the whole world as their audience, and global media signals than transgress national boundaries. More and more people have access to some form of broadcast signal so that in the 1990s it may well become true that the "whole world is watching" television and some form of international news provision.

At the same time, forces of localization include religio-ethnic conflicts; the increasing self-expression of other minorities; and, in communications, the rise of many kinds of "small media" including ethnic media; exile media; immigrant media; and alternative, participatory, grassroots media, which often provide dissident readings of the news as provided by the big players. In a similar polarization, there is on the one hand an ever more apparent globalization of international news providers, especially television news, while on the other hand, international news provision seems to be more and more mediated by regional and local gate-keepers.

Again, new technologies make it ever easier to edit television text, to add a different voice over, in essence to cook up a news story with a very different inflection than the raw material received from a television news agency. And while there is considerable concentration at the top amongst the global players, there is a significant diversification of smaller news-providers also.

In between the global and the local there are the emergent regional structures, Europe being one of the most significant as a political and economic, dependent on a certain degree of historical amnesia to overcome not-so-distant conflicts. If it has not yet reached a successful construction of a new imagery of identification, a pan-regional acceptance of being "European", certainly the development of a fierce boundary-definition process is well in hand with the growth of "Fortress Europe" discourse and strict immigration policy.

New(s) Maps and New(s) Agendas

Since international news coverage has often had a very close connection to the prevailing attitudes toward international relations even in societies with the "freest" presses, a mediated news map provides indication of emerging trends in international relations. It would also show whether the geographic regionalism evidence in older studies is now reinforced, or whether there are new criteria of selection of news stories emerging, using notions of "cultural proximity" such as Islam, for example, that work to construct a cultural, not geographic, map of relations. Given the problems of levels of analysis that globalization theory has thrown up-the leakiness of the nation-state system; the emergence of the global in actors, culture, news stories; regionalism; the return to the local-it seems a pertinent moment to reanalyse the emergent geography of international news.

A few media researchers have tried at various times to map the diverse news geographies of national media systems. Most recently a one-day snap-shot of international news was organized by the ICC; the results were evocative, but the project was not sufficiently elaborate or coherently devised to provide much systematic information.

Perspectives on the News Process

In order to provide an understanding of the place of news flow studies within the overall field of international news research it is useful to distinguish between the level of analysis, i.e., micro or macro analysis, and between the kind of perspective that is applied on the news process, i.e. how is the social process of international news conceptualized. International news has been dominated by two perspectives on the news process: the perspective of selection and the perspective of construction. Studies using a perspective of selection traditionally focuses on the news 'event'.

The events of the world are the independent variable that determines the structure of foreign news. The social institutions play a secondary, intermediate role as 'selector' or gatekeeper; they perform functions like selection, rejection, re-editing etc. Closely related to the concept of selection is the idea of transportation. The social process of making international news is about the distribution, i.e., physical transportation, of news items.

The perspective of construction looks at the news process from the opposite direction: news is a social artifact. Social conventions and practices, specific values, and the specific allocation of material resources work together to produce a specific outcome: news. The social institution is the primary variable; the form, content and volume of news are all a product of the social practices of the news institutions. In table 1 these two perspectives have been paired with the micro-macro distinction, thus providing a matrix of four approaches to the analysis of international news.

In the first approach, micro level and construction perspective, we find empirical studies of news content, often comparative case studies like "US and Arab press coverage of UN negotiations". In both cases the underlying assumption is that social institutions heavily influence the form, content and volume of news.

Table 1

Four approaches to the study of international news

	Perspective of construction	Perspective of selection
Micro level	Ideology critique of news content Analysis of organizations	Gatekeeper analysis
Macro level	Media imperialism Political economy of news media	News flow analysis

In the second approach, macro level and construction perspective, we generally find more theoretical contributions concerned with the question of media imperialism. The school on the political economy of communication has also provided some insights to the field of international news research. In the third approach, micro level and selection perspective, we find the oldest tradition, the gatekeeper analysis. Although severe criticism has been raised against the gatekeeper approach during the last two decades, it hasn't completely lost ground. Especially in the research field of international news the idea of gatekeeping is still very much alive. The concept of gatekeeping intuitively corresponds to some basic empirical observations at the micro level, i.e., the newsroom: foreign news is brought into the newsroom, something is selected, rewritten, etc.

Furthermore, the most influential theoretical contribution to the study of international news, is very much influenced by a selection and gatekeeper perspective. In the fourth approach, macro level and selection perspective, we finally find the news flow analyses. The matrix in Table 1 is of course a crude generalization; some of the studies of international news are more tightly confined to a single approach than others. Also news flow studies have frequently involved other approaches and have for instance successfully been combined with organizational studies. However, the matrix useful, because it provides a framework for distinguishing between different conceptualizations of the news process that predominantly have been connected to specific kinds of research on international news.

News flow analysis, including TV news flow analysis, has been conducted as a macro level analysis. Generally the idea has been to locate and specify a few general and pervasive characteristics of international news at a global level, to map the global condition so to speak.

News flow analysis has implicitly or explicitly understood the news process to be a question about selection, at least in a very general sense of the term; for empirical analysis the point of departure has been a simple, but important observation: international news and television news pictures are transported around the globe between countries and between social actors and the volume and content of this flow is continuously subject to a kind of selection process: something is added, removed or changed from the flow depending on the countries and actors involved.

The application of these metaphors of transportation and selection to the understanding of news is not without problems, but for now will take a simple and positive position: Yes, transportation and selection are useful metaphors; TV news footage, for instance, is actually transported around the globe every minute and during this process the footage is constantly subject to selection.

TV news flow studies

In the following will focus on the studies done on the flow of international television news. In particular pay attention to the studies that have considered the flow of pictorial material, i.e., video news footage in either "raw", unedited form or finished form, i.e., edited news items ready to be broadcast. If we use the transportation/selection metaphor to inform understanding of the flow of international television news we can distinguish between different steps or stages in the flow of news. In the real world these steps are overlapping and interdependent but for our analytical purpose we can make a logical distinction between four steps:

1) The flow of news items between actors at the whole-sale level, i.e., between news agencies and other exchange mechanisms like Eurovision, Asiavision and some similar organizations.
2) The flow of news items between actors at the whole-sale level and actors at the retail-level, i.e., the distribution of agency material to the newsroom of national, regional or international broadcasters and the syndication by agencies of pictures that are produced by broadcasters.
3) The flow of news items between actors at the retail level, i.e., the exchange or sale of news items between the broadcasters themselves.
4) The flow of news items from the broadcasters to the audiences, i.e., the reception process of international news.

The majority of studies consists of comparative analyses of the output of broadcast news; typically you find quantitative studies of content or geographical origin that compare the foreign news of two or more national broadcasters. These studies do of course provide interesting and useful information about differences between the output of national broadcasters. However, such studies only indirectly reveal information about the actual volume and content of TV news flows between nations and actors.

They do not take into account the many different steps in the process and the different actors and factors involved that influence the final output. As a consequence the process of news flow is left unexplained. Without some elaborated theory or model of the news flow process to inform the interpretation of data this kind of data really doesn't say much about the flow of news pictures between nations or actors. Such data may be interesting from other perspectives but for the understanding of news flow they are of limited value. It's really like trying to understand the ecological system of the sea by counting the number of fish you can catch from the shore.

A few studies have tried to analyze the content and volume of the television news items that are actually exchanged between actors at the wholesale level and between wholesale level and retail level. Taken together these few studies also reveal that few-if any-general conclusions can be drawn about the character of TV news flow at the global level.

The studies seem to indicate that stable or uniform patterns of news flow are to be located at a lower level, i.e. depending on the region, the historical period and the specific actors involved. For instance, the idea that international TV news flow would be a "one-way traffic", as find only support in some of the studies and are actually contradicted by some of the findings of the newer studies.

The final step in the TV news flow, the consumption of foreign TV news by audiences, has typically been completely outside the scope of news flow analysis, theoretically as well as empirically. The implicit assumption has been that the structure of the broadcaster's supply of foreign news somehow would be copied by the audience.

Inequalities of volume and content would be transferred directly to the minds of audiences. Developments in reception studies have certainly challenged such assumptions but the tradition of news flow studies has been rather slow to integrate such knowledge. Some studies of foreign TV news reception are now in the pipeline, for instance the "News of the World"-project headed by Klaus Bruhn Jensen, University of Copenhagen, and these will help to fill the gap concerning the fourth step in the flow process.

Generally speaking there has been too little work done on the news flow at the wholesale level. This is of course not only a result of conceptual or methodological problems, but also due to the practical and financial difficulties for researchers to get access to the actors and feed-points at the wholesale level. But whatever the reasons are, the simple fact remains that our knowledge about the flow of international television news at the whole-sale level is very limited.

Correspondingly very little work has been done on the organizational and editorial structure of commercial TV news sellers. Some work has been done on the European public TV news exchange system Eurovision, but knowledge about the activities and structure of TV news agencies is very scarce. Some books have been written about the agencies of printed news but these studies hardly deal with the TV dimension. The television news agency dimension is a black box in the understanding of international television news flow.

There are three major problems in the ways earlier research has interpreted data. Firstly, you often find a conceptual change when news flow analyses move from the stage of empirical analysis to the stage of interpretation and theoretical explanation. In order to explain news flow patterns a shift often occurs from selection to construction perspective.

The news flow patterns are often explained by concepts borrowed from theories of media and cultural imperialism, political economy or dependency theory. But little work has been done to mediate between the selection-transportation perspective of the empirical flow studies and the construction perspective of the theoretical explanations.

There are very few attempts to explain how these macro social structures actually determine or influence the shaping of news flow patterns. How does media imperialism, for instance, actually work at the level of social actors, for instance in the newsroom of TV news agencies, whose actions at the micro level together result in the observable news flow patterns?

Until now news flow analysis has either been rather narrow empirical counting of news items or macro theoretical explanation of these findings. What is missing is a theoretical framework that can create a common ground between general social structure and the social actors actually involved in the micro social actions that together create the discernable news flow patterns.

Secondly, it is fair to say-and that it must be said openly-that often there have been drawn too extensive conclusions on existing news flow data. Especially moral and political interpretations and conclusions have been drawn too early without a thorough examination of evidence that could support other conclusions or at least limit the reach of one's own propositions.

Take the case of international news agencies. During the debate in the 1970s about the New World Information and Communication Order much criticism was raised against the activities of agencies-and similarly many voices were raised in defense of the agencies by western politicians, the agencies themselves, etc. Both of these political positions were supported by research findings.

The agencies, for instance, were criticized for providing news of a very sensational nature and for providing a much too biased coverage of events in third world countries. In the case of television the agencies were criticized for visualizing the third world countries on western terms and not as the countries themselves would depict their internal situation.

Foreign TV news flow in Western Europe indicates that the agency material used by public broadcasters in general is of a more narrow political-and serious-nature than the material produced by the public broadcasters themselves.

The television agencies often rely on material produced by other actors; actually, one of the most frequent critiques raised by public broadcasters in Western Europe against the agencies is that they produce too little material themselves and rely too much on footage produced by other broadcasters. So the footage depicting a 3rd world news event that is accused for giving a too Eurocentric or American interpretation of the event may in some cases have been shot by a local camera crew. Some findings can-and must in some cases-be used in the political debate, and researchers should rather be conscious and explicit about these political implications and use this knowledge constructively in their work - than naively try to avoid any normative 'infection'.

Thirdly, and closely related to the second problem, the interpretations of data have been guided by a theoretical position that considered the international news flow to be structured by a rather limited set of factors. To put it more bluntly: both the realm of foreign news and the outside social world have been considered to be much more simple and homogeneous than is really the case.

In particular the connection between the operations of media and external social forces has been considered to be a rather simple one. Explanations of news flow patterns seldom go into consideration of the more specific and to some extent independent features of media institutions: the editorial practices, journalistic education, the role of technology, conventions of expression, etc. But an understanding of news flow patterns needs-ideally-to take all these different factors into account.

In practice would of course have to limit the number of factors and aspects that are dealt with in any one study, but what is just as obvious is that a multi-disciplinary approach is needed in order to explain news flow data. Especially it is needed to bridge the gap between social science and human science traditions: Foreign news is both a discursive-symbolic and social practice and both dimensions must be taken into account.

The study of international news flows will be even more complicated in the future. Take the case of television news flow. The volume of this flow expands rapidly almost all over the world not least as a result of the proliferation of satellite technology. At the same time the actors multiply and change character. For instance the dividing line between wholesale and retail level is getting blurred. Agencies begin to deliver complete TV news programme packages ready for broadcast and broadcasters set up transnational services that both function as agencies and as traditional broadcast services.

The agencies also broaden their activities and go, for instance, more directly into public relation work, production of Video News Releases etc. The genre of television news has ramified into several sub-genres like business news, entertainment news, updates, live-news, breakfast news, etc. This calls for more sensitive analysis; collection of data, interpretations and model building must have a more refined character in the future.

The following suggestions for a new approach to the study of international news flow are not in any way meant to be a prescription or handbook, a new theory or methodology of news flow analysis. On the contrary what is needed is not any orthodoxy but a whole range of different kinds of analyses of international news. What we want is rather to plea for a general change in perspective and a shift in analytical level in order to overcome some of the shortcomings of earlier analyses, in particular the problems related to the interpretation and explanation of news flow patterns.

The idea is to mediate between both axes in the matrix presented in table 1. This is done by introducing a new conceptualization of the news process called the perspective of interaction and insert the middle range as the primary level of analysis. This new combination, middle range and perspective of interaction, is presented in Table 2.

The alternative to macro-level analysis and theory is certainly not a postmodern celebration of differences, endless variation or only local truths. The alternative is rather a call for careful reflection about the level at which we can expect to find systematic structures, i.e., stable patterns of interaction. This cannot, of course, only be solved theoretically but must also be examined through empirical analysis. For instance, by examining existing studies of television news flow it seems to that at the regional level, i.e. continent or sub-continent, in some cases find stable patterns of news flow, but such a specification must of course be related to other factors.

Table 2. A new approach to the study of international news

Perspective of interaction		
	Empirical studies:	
	Time:	Historical changes

	Space:	Regional specificity
	Actor:	News sources, journalists, agencies audiences etc.
Middle range:	*Theoretical studies*	The development of more complex models that allow us to understand and explain news flow patterns as outcome of interaction between different factors: technical, aesthetic, journalistic institution, general societal development, etc

The observable news flow patterns are gross summaries of the outcome of numerous kinds of social interactions that each have a different motivation and outcome. Actors anticipate and monitor the action of others and continuously adjust their own action according to that knowledge. They do not only follow their own interests; but in order to pursue these interests they accommodate to the actual circumstances of the specific social interaction. Thus the analysis cannot stop with an identification of the different interests of involved actors but must go on and consider the outcome as a result of an interaction, that typically can be described as a negotiation or exchange between the actors and their interests.

The perspective of selection took the news to be initially given: news or news events are simply there and the question is what happens to them afterwards. The perspective of construction took the social institution to be initially given: social structures are simply there and the question is how these structures determine the volume and content of news. According to the construction perspective news is like a tabula rasa; it is solely a product of the journalistic institution.

The selection and construction perspectives are rather deterministic-they cannot explain how news is both institutionally organized and continuously open for change and variation. The perspective of interaction, that is very much inspired by the structuration theory of Anthony Giddens, can overcome some of this determinism, because it allows us to examine how the social actors both are informed by general social structures and accommodate/ interpret these structures according to the specific kind of social interaction they are engaged in and this process of interpretation or accommodation is exactly what allows for social change.

The proposed framework is very general and of course applicable to other kinds of news and media studies. The mid-life crisis of news flow studies will hopefully not end in resignation or despair; there is still an urgent need to document, analyse and explain the patterns of international news flow. If news flow analysis downgrades some of its more youthful global pretensions and upgrades the theoretical work, the mid-life crisis could be succeeded by an invigoration of the field.

Media Criticism

The idea is based on the logic that, while the media have a great influence in society, they also enjoy an exceptional degree of freedom, along with respective accountability. And one of many media accountability systems is media criticism. The kind of media criticism advocated by the media monitoring idea is not politically motivated interest group advocacy but scientifically based description and assessment of media performance carried out by methods of content analysis. The section outlines international networking of research groups committed to pooling together the evidence of countless national studies so as to facilitate a worldwide review of media performance.

The growing tendency for the ownership of the means of communication and information to pass into the hands of either governments or multinational. In this connection MacBride comments that "it would be very useful to devise some system for monitoring the extent to which certain newspapers and chains of newspapers distort news concerning disarmament in the world". 1983 the Mass Media Declaration of Unesco was five years old, and Sean MacBride addressed in Paris in November 1983 a ceremony commemorating this landmark document of international communication. He made a strong point about media concentration and called upon professionals and scholars to trace and document this phenomenon, which was working against the positive trend of the time that MacBride used to characterize as a "shift in the centre of gravity of power from governments, from established authorities to public opinion."

On that occasion MacBride did not go on to recommend a system of monitoring media performance simply because the idea was not yet articulated. Actually, the first sketchy notes on it were put on paper during that reception by the present author together with MacBride and the chief of Unesco's Division for Free Flow of Information and Communication Policies, Hamdy Kandil. On that basis a short memorandum was drafted outlining the idea in terms of two levels: first, scientific groundwork by pooling together empirical evidence of content analysis concerning the media coverage of global problems such as peace and war, and secondly, a commission of internationally known public figures to issue an annual review and assessment of the overall media performance.

A rough estimate of financial resources needed to get such a system established, not counting the actual content analysis work which was supposed to be nationally funded, was 50 000 U.S. dollars a year-something that at the time seemed realistically could be raised from Unesco and/or the UN. This informal memo served as a reference when MacBride met the UN Secretary General Perez de Cuellar in early 1984 and raised the monitoring idea, among other things-with a generally positive response.

Then, in the summer of 1984, Johan Galtung paid one of his seasonal visits to Finland (addressing a seminar of the Finnish peace movement), and he was consulted on the idea by the present author. Galtung reacted enthusiastically and invited a planning workshop to his then base, a free university in Paris in spring 1985, but this offer could not be acted upon by the intended core group due to timing problems.

Moreover, the United States announced at the end of 1984 its intention to withdraw from Unesco within one year, and that spread an atmosphere of caution and controversy around everything related to Unesco's communication program. MacBride especially was of the opinion that one would be ill advised to go ahead with the idea for the time being.

However, in 1986—the International Year of Peace-MacBride was already prepared to raise the idea in his Foreword to the NIICO Sourcebook. By that time he, like many others, had come to the conclusion that it was pointless to wait for Unesco to come along. In a more general sense, the intergovernmental structures were seen as increasingly doubtful partners. Instead, non-governmental organizations (NGOs) appeared as more and more relevant carriers of initiatives such as the "monitoring project" and the MacBride Round Table a couple of years later. It was a move away from established political structures-state and capital in Galtung's triangle-towards the civil society.

It should be added that two related initiatives emerged around 1990, promoted independent of the like-minded activists. First, George Gerbner started what is called the "Cultural Environment Movement" (CEM) in the United States, based on his cultural indicators research and turned into a grassroots movement reflecting the media consumers' interests.

The CEM is also preparing a "Covenant of Peoples' Communication Rights" and a "Viewers' Declaration of Independence" for a major CEM conference in St.Louis in 1996. Finally, to complete the background-and to demonstrate that this is not just an isolated idea entertained by advocates such as MacBride, Gerbner, Hamelink and Nordenstreng-it is worth recalling a paragraph from the chapter by Alfred Balk, former editor of Columbia Journalism Review and World Press Review, included in an anthology on media freedom and accountability based on a seminar held at the Gannett Center for Media Studies at Columbia University in 1986.

The idea has a simple four-step logic which proceeds along the following path: First, the mass media play a vital role in (post)modern societies and in the surrounding global culture which makes them a backbone of a pervasive cultural environment—the media have Influence.

This influence is today greater than at the time of the MacBride Commission, since the 'media reality' has gained ground from conventional reality especially in political life. And the problem is made especially serious by the fact that this mediated reality can be bought-unlike conventional reality.

Accordingly, the first step in this reasoning about media monitoring assumes that the mass media continue to be important in the world as instruments to address vast audiences and to shape public and private minds at the national and international levels. This means that, contrary to what many today suggest, new media techologies will not bring about an end of MASS media and an "end of journalism." Surely, new means and practices emerge, but the basic characteristics of mass comunication seem to remain and even increase in socio-cultural influence.

Second, the mass media, in particular the printed press, enjoy a special constitutional status which, gives them protection against much of conventional social policies-the media have Freedom.

This freedom is a vital element in a democratic society a safeguard of human rights in civil society. Therefore the special constitutional status of the media and its freedom must be respected and defended as an essential part of the monitoring idea.

Third, the mass media not only enjoy an exceptional degree of autonomy but also carry duties and responsibilities (based on the same international instruments) which call for normative regulation of this sphere of cultural ecology, both on legal and ethical levels—the media have Accountability.

This accountability is part and parcel of the same special constitutional status which grants freedom to the media. It would be both sociologically and politically naive to place media outside of any social controls. Accountability can conceptually be divided into various levels and aspects, including law and ethics.

The aspect related to the present monitoring idea is focussed on an analytical appreciation of the media content, thus largely bypassing all the well-known normative and structural aspects, including those media accountability systems that are implemented through professional codes of ethics or media councils. Thus the monitoring being pursued here has a limited scope-limited but still significant if its potential is fully utilized.

Fourth, the mass media are being regulated by legal and financial means to a degree determined by the political balance of power prevailing in each society, and there is little that the professional and academic community can do about it, but there is an untapped potential for indirect participation in the democratic process of media accountability-through Media Criticism.

The media criticism called upon here is not the kind of more or less politically motivated interest group advocacy that is well known everywhere. What is meant here is scientifically based description and assessment of media performance, mainly carried out by methods of content analysis. And the epistemological paradigm is one of conventional realism rather than postmodern phenomenalism. Thus it is assumed that an objective reality exists and it can be discovered more or less accurately, although in practice the media coverage may be far removed from true reality. In other words, the reasoning typically follows the correspondence theory of truth: comparing media coverage with extra-media data.

On the other hand, truth checking can be left aside and monitoring may be focussed on tracing the trends and interests of the content alone-the ideological narrative of the media discourse along the new tradition of cultural studies. There exists a lot of content analysis, especially as case studies, and in some instances like the Gulf War there is a huge accumulation of evidence from numerous small and large works, both national and international.

The problem is, however, that these exercises are seldom pooled together so as to facilitate an overall review and assessment of media performance-neither in one country nor internationally. If done on a permanent basis such overviews would help to identify neglected areas not only in media coverage but also in studies of media content, which are too often based on a haphazard choice of topic and media.

In such a manner one could counteract the tendency to end up with abundant piles of disjointed data and one could also encourage young scholars to focus on content areas which are strategically important given the research carried out so far.

Speaking of media criticism, it has practically no tradition in journalism in the same sense as in the fields of film, music and other areas of performing arts-not to speak of literature, the basis of literary criticism and aesthetics. As a matter of fact, it is a challenge for journalism research to give better shape and recognition to what already has been exercised in some places under labels such as media education or media analysis. In this respect journals such as the Columbia Journalism Review, American Journalism Review and Extra! constitute a good reference point.

This rationale not only rendered support to a "monitoring project" but it even called forth, indeed demanded, some sort of an institutionalized accountability system. The system called forth was not a legal or administrative mechanism by official powers but something that falls within the sphere of non-governmental civil society.

On the other hand, the system called forth was not another form of straight self-regulation of the media, since the content analysis was supposed to be carried out by independent scholars and the overall media performance was supposed to be assessed by panels which would also be relatively independent from the media-otherwise the idea of accountability would be missed.

Obviously this is a line which is quite similar to the reasoning by the Hutchins Commission already half a century ago. No doubt the same rationale is more or less shared by other similar initiatives such as the above-mentioned Cultural Environment Movement and Peoples' Communication Charter. These initiatives do not only reflect narrow academic or social interests but should rather be taken as indicators of a fundamental tendency in contemporary society whereby the ever larger role played by the media inevitably leads to reconsideration of the ways in which their accountability is defined and monitored. A strong political signal to this effect came in 1993 from the Council of Europe whose Parliamentary Assembly passed a resolution and recommendation on the ethics of journalism.

While scientific content analysis constitutes a cornerstone of the "monitoring project" it does not suggest new, elaborate and expensive research to be done before anything else. It is taken for granted that a lot of content analytical research is being carried out all over the world in any case-as Master's theses and Doctoral dissertations by students, academic contributions by scholars, administrative exercises by authorities, and in some cases as international joint ventures. A notable example of last-mentioned type of research is "World of the News" carried out by the International Association for Mass Communication Research (IAMCR) for Unesco in the early 1980s.

The monitoring idea does not advocate any more such cumbersome works which tend to consume a lot of mental and material energy, often with little outcome. Instead it is strongly suggested to organize the pooling together of existing research and to invest the energies into the digesting of such an accumulated research evidence.

As a matter of fact, much content analysis evidence is lost in the absence of an international system of pooling, accumulating and comparing data from innumerous national case studies which typically focus on a limited topic or time period. Taken together such research evidence provides a great potential "to appraise and report annually upon the performance of the press". Indeed, a global overview of media performance based on content analysis evidence would help the students and scholars in the field to better place their particular problems in an overall perspective.

One might also self-critically observe that few fields of science have been as sterile in terms of assessing social and global responsibilities as has been the case with communication research, not least content analysis. Where natural scientists are raising their voice regarding environmental problems and medical scientists continuously assess problems of human health, communication scientists should have a natural role in taking stock of media performance-not only in isolated cases but also as a global issue, nationally and internationally.

So far there have been surprisingly few contributions in this field that address the question in a truly global manner. For example, when there was a need to assess what impact the Mass Media Declaration of Unesco had brought to the field ten years later in 1988, it turned out that there was little cumulative research to count on.

On the other hand, Global Glasnost by Galtung and Vincent provides an exemplary demonstration of what can be done by capitalizing on a host of empirical data from existing literature combined with insightful theory and ethic. The rationale explained here by no means suggests to undermine structural factors behind and beyond media content. It admits-just like MacBride did when the idea was born-that there is a need for similar, indeed parallel, monitoring of media concentration, consumption, etc. But as pointed out above, the rationale is based on a firm belief that mass-mediated content constitutes a strategic part of broader reasoning about the media-their freedom and accountability, ultimately their role in democracy.

Consequently, the idea is not particularly new or radical. Rather at issue is a classic question of journalism-paradoxically neglected in the prevailing tradition of media theory and practice.

Monitoring Media Performance

Obviously the monitoring of media performance is an idea whose time has come. It does not need any UN or Unesco resolutions for implementation; it is evolving quite independently of governmental and intergovernmental structures. On the other hand, the idea is being promoted by governmental concerns such as those currently prevailing in Europe in relation to racism and xenophobia.

Both the Council of Europe and the European Union have programs to encourage media and journalists to combat these phenomena and to support an atmosphere of tolerance in society.

As a matter of fact, the media coverage of race, ethnic minorities and symptoms of intolerance such as xenophobia has become recognized as a social problem by politicians and professionals alike. It is logical, then, that the International Federation of Journalists (IFJ) proceeded in 1994 to establish, with the support of the Council of Europe and the European Union, a working group against racism and xenophobia-something that would have been unthinkable still a decade ago. And one of the priority activities pursued by the IFJ working group is precisely media monitoring more or less in the sense advocated here.

The IFJ monitoring project will be pursued first and foremost in Europe, with highlights such as an international journalism prize for combating racism and xenophobia. It will be supported by a parallel academic works which has grown out of the IAMCR working group on ethnicity, racism and the media coordinated by Charles Husband (ERaM) as well as the action program proposed by Teun van Dijk.

Thus the idea is moving ahead along two tracks: professional and academic. Significantly, there is little or no friction between the two; they seem to support each other, unlike many previous cooperative efforts. Yet there is a recognition that the two should remain distinct, or else there is a risk that professional journalists would no longer be actively engaged, but would instead turn defensive with well known arguments about freedom suppressed by outside forces-including academic forces with their intellectual challenge.

Another impressive indication about the timeliness of the monitoring idea comes from the circles concerned about the representation and portrayal of women in news media.

January 18, 1995 was chosen as an "ordinary" newsday when activists in 70 countries recorded the main outlets of newspapers, radio and television news, coding the stories, and people in them, using over 20 common variables. The "Global Media Monitoring Project" is being coordinated by the Canadian MediaWatch organization and its results will be reported to the Fourth World Conference on Women convened by the UN in Beijing in September 1995.

Although this media monitoring was limited to one day only, the number of participating countries makes it still perhaps the largest exercise of comparative content analysis ever carried out. Moreover, participation in this exercise was voluntary, which demonstrates how spontaneous interest can be mobilized around a good cause and with the help of an informal network.

The global women's monitoring as well as the European work on race and intolerance show how the idea proposed may materialize thematically instead of as an overall survey embracing various global issues at one time.

Other currently attractive themes, in addition to gender and race, are environment and disarmament-the latter a topic which MacBride and others started to pursue more than a decade ago. The implementation may occur spontaneously or with the support of a political niche in some thematic cases, but a true materialization of the monitoring idea needs something more. It needs a worldwide network of collaborating scholarly activists.

8

Organisational Effectiveness of Media

There is always the danger of sounding pretentious when putting forward an allegedly "new" or "fresh" alternative perspective within the vast and highly theorised domain of "communication studies". In this instance, the risk has to be taken for a variety of reasons. For one thing, the adult communication management approach does not sit comfortably with the conventional divisions within the boundaries of contemporary communication theory. In effect, the "adult communication management" perspective crosses the traditional boundaries which appear to separate interpersonal from organisational or instructional communication.

Another important difference between the adult communication management (ACM) perspective and existing theoretical frameworks within the field of human communication is that adult communication management theory draws from a number of diverse disciplinary approaches and backgrounds. As such, adult communication management theory is both multidisciplinary and eclectic. It is not grounded solely in social interpretive theory, nor exclusively in psychologically oriented thinking, although it would be true to say that there is a strong leaning toward psychologically determined views of the world.

Adult communication management is that, unlike several other contemporary theories of human communication, it does not derive its rationale exclusively from "communication" literature. It has been suggested that the field of communication studies is not grounded in any single discipline but is rather a multidisciplinary field characterised by a number of issues and debates. Some of these issues and debates appear to hold minimal interest for scholars in specialised areas of the communication studies field. For this reason, adult communication management is a selective perspective, concentrating on a set of issues relevant to the way people communicate with each other in various kinds of systems and organisations.

Finally, it may be worth emphasising that the adult communication management perspective is characterised by a distinctly applied nature. Although it purports to have very general applications, because most graduate students undertaking study in this area have been actively involved in adult and/or vocational education, this perspective has been quite deliberately associated with the adult vocational education field of practice. Nevertheless, there is no necessary reason as to why adult communication management should not be extended to any work-related contexts in which people need to communicate with each other.

One simple way of understanding the thrust of the adult communication management perspective is to separate the two key contributing concepts in the term. In this way, it is evident that the focus is specifically on adults rather than children. This is not to say, however, that, adult communication management theory is predicated on the assumption that adults invariably learn and communicate differently from non-adults. Nevertheless, the development of a parallel perspective on child communication management may also be warranted.

The words "communication management" are used in a particular sense in this perspective. Essentially, communication management refers to the ways in which communicating individuals construct, coordinate, and clarify their meanings about their interpersonal worlds. There is also a suggestion here that if reciprocity occurs, that is to say, when individuals are communicating with each other on the basis of mutually developed understandings, these individuals are displaying some form of communication competence.

At this point, it is important to note that within the adult communication management perspective, traditional conceptions and definitions of communication management are seen to be somewhat limiting. Communication managers would be able to influence the quality, quantity, timing and form of messages received by organisational units. Thus, "communication managers" were conceived to be individuals who controlled the flow of information among the various members of systems or organisations.

The view espoused in the adult communication management perspective is that all individuals within systems exercise some form of communication management, albeit in varying degrees of intensity, opportunity, or skill. Clearly, some people, because of the nature of their jobs, spend relatively large proportions of their time in interacting with others. Alternatively, there are inevitably persons who, by virtue of the tasks assigned to them, are not required to meet as frequently with colleagues from other departments, divisions, or sections of their particular systems.

Regardless of these evident differences, every individual within a system is potentially a "communication manager". This is a bit like saying that any person within a system is potentially a leader when the system provides opportunities for worker participation in corporate decision-making. As it has been suggested, "anyone who contributes in any way to the accomplishment of the goals of the system participates in system-oriented individual leadership". Like participative leadership, therefore, communication management within systems is characterised by the interdependence of all members of the system.

There are several important assumptions upon which the conceptual framework of adult communication management theory rests. In part, these assumptions relate to ways in which adults learn about and perceive their social worlds. Complementing these, however, are assumptions about the nature and performance of communication management by people within systems.

Assumptions about Adult Learning and Perception

Whilst it may be true, as has already been suggested, that hypothesised distinctions between the ways adults and non-adults learn are less convincing today than two decades ago, there are grounds for assuming that adults perceive their worlds differently from the ways children do. The noted genetic epistemologist Jean Piaget, developed a collection of data to substantiate his claim that the child's construction of reality is qualitatively different from that of the adult. In part, this difference could be accounted for by the powerful tendency of children to think animistically when confronted with seemingly mysterious and inexplicable phenomena or events, whereas adults would typically look for a "logical" or commonsense reason. Assumption 1, therefore, is that in general adults view their worlds differently from the ways in which children do.

The Piagetian literature also emphasises the developmental nature of thinking. According to Piaget, individuals progress through stages of cognitive development from infancy to adulthood. Each stage is characterised by qualitatively different ways of reasoning and of viewing the world. Thus, whereas children typically explain their experience of their worlds egocentrically and through concrete modes of thought, the thinking of adults is characterised by reciprocity, or the ability to see things from someone else's viewpoint as well as from one's own. In addition, adults are assumed to have reached the stage of "formal operations" in which one's thinking is determined by the ability to exercise logic and to reason in propositional form.

Thus, Assumption 2 is that adults are able to reason and think in ways which do not typify the reasoning and thinking of children. Whilst it is not denied that some children may be capable of reasoning in relatively sophisticated ways, in general, children's thinking is assumed to be more concrete rather than abstract in nature.

Another critical difference between the ways adults and children learn and perceive their worlds relates to the significance of personal experience as a basis for knowing, acting, and communicating. It is probably true that all people learn a great deal through experience. The more experience people have, the more they are able to capitalise on it and use it to guide their communication with and behaviour toward others. Obviously, children rely on a more limited range of experiences than adults do. For this reason, Assumption 3 is that adults rely considerably more on experience as a basis for learning than do children.

Whilst there is a strong relationship between experience and learning, particularly in the case of adults, the connection between learning and communication suggests that experience influences the ways in which individuals communicate. Especially for adults, experience provides a means for both learning and communicating. In the latter case, adults use their interpersonal experiences to form impressions of individuals who enter their social worlds. These experiences become part of a cognitive structure which enables communicating individuals to establish, stabilise, develop, or terminate relationships with others.

Finally, it should be noted that a legitimate goal of adult learning is the attainment of some form of autonomy and self-direction. Whilst the communicative behaviour of adults may broadly be categorised in terms of needs for interdependence, adult learning may be said to be progressing in a direction from facilitator or teacher control to that of personal or self-control. It has been argued, moreover, that personal control is strongly associated with the notion of "communicator" (or "communicative") competence. Assumption 4, therefore, is that a major goal of adult learners is the development of their ability to be self-directed.

Much of the adult communication management perspective is focused on how adults communicate with each other in the workplace. Just as children spend a substantial portion of their normal days in school rooms, adults occupy most of their salaried or career time in different kinds of organisations and work settings. The nature of these occupational systems to a large extent affect the type of interpersonal communication which is likely to eventuate amongst the members of these systems. On this basis, Assumption 5 is that the communication between adults in work settings differs qualitatively from the communication between children in formal instructional settings.

It is equally important, however, to recognise that adult-adult communication will differ from one kind of system or organisational setting to another. The extent to which systems are open, flexible, hierarchical or "flat" in their management structures constitutes a basis for identifying the nature and effectiveness of communication among the adults in those particular systems. Thus, Assumption 6 is that communication between adults in one system or organisation may differ both qualitatively and quantitatively from patterns or forms of communication between adults in other systems.

Although there are characteristics common to all interpersonal systems, the differences relate to the amount of communication between adults and the quality of that communication. Organisations whose mission statements focus on productivity to the exclusion of "quality of life" considerations, very often create a climate of adversarial and competitive communication. On the other hand, systems whose focus is on people and their needs, are often perceived by persons both from within and beyond as encouraging constructive and profitable dialogue among members.

Whilst some scholars continue to refer to "acts" of communication, adult communication management theory prefers to regard communication as a process. An "act of communication" suggests that the communicative event is very much self-contained with, moreover, a clear beginning and a definable point of conclusion. Not all communicative events, however, fall neatly into the classification of "acts". Alternatively, where they can be identified as "acts", the sum of several such acts could well be seen as forming a chain within a more global process.

Such a global process, moreover, may not have an evident endpoint. Instead, the communication process may be presumed to continue beyond the point of one's ability to experience it. The communication process, therefore, may consist of episodes of interpersonal contact at certain times. Nevertheless, the likelihood of future interpersonal encounters suggests that the communication process is continuous rather than a discrete unit of dialogue between interacting individuals.

Take the example of a group facilitator leading a collection of adult learners in a question and answer session. Each interchange between the facilitator and some individual learner could be construed as a single, separate "act" of communication. Nevertheless, when a sequence of such acts is put together, it is possible to conceptualise this sequence as one instructional episode consisting of interactions between combinations of different people present at the time. In addition, the possibility of future interactions is not precluded since it is very likely that there will be future meetings between the learner and facilitator. Such future meetings would naturally link strongly with the sequences of previous interpersonal encounters and experiences.

Adult communication management theory does not aim to atomise human communication or behaviour. It is not a theory supportive of the notion of "frames of human behaviour" as the units of analysis. Instead, the focus is essentially on communication as a holistic process. In other words, understanding the nature of human communication involves an appreciation of the context in which individuals relate and the location of that relationship within the complex of all possible relationships between people in their particular systems. Hence, Assumption 7 is that human communication is conceived as a continuous process rather than as a discrete act.

Adult communication management theory also accepts the well established notions that interpersonal communication is inevitable and that it is the most pervasive of all forms of communication. Whilst these notions are seen as axiomatic, they do signal the all-embracing nature of interpersonal communication which may be explained and understood in terms of many generalisable, comprehensive principles, concepts, and rules. Based on this line of reasoning, Assumption 8 is that interpersonal communication is at the core of all forms of human communication.

Arguably, therefore, contemporary scholarly literature and research in interpersonal communication should be incorporated in the rationale of any human communication theoretical perspective. Consistent with this claim, adult communication management acknowledges, within its conceptual framework, the centrality of interpersonal communication theory. It is emphasised, however, that such a theoretical core must be complemented by a mechanism or structure for understanding the nature and effects of contextual variables on how interacting adults manage communication processes. Thus, Assumption 9 is that human communication processes need to be understood in terms of the contexts in which they occur.

There are three significant contributing perspectives to adult communication management theory. The first is the interpersonal perspective which represents the theoretical core since it is fundamental to all forms of human communication. It is assumed, moreover, that the interpersonal communication processes described in this section, apply to all situations where individuals interact with other persons and where people's communication and behaviours are largely shaped by their perceptions of the quality of their relationships and communication with others. Essentially, the interpersonal perspective derives from the social cognition domain, and more particularly from concepts central to constructivist theory.

The second contributing perspective focuses on the context of human communication. Within this orientation, it is possible to determine both how the setting can influence the way individuals communicate with others, and how individuals, by the ways they communicate, can influence the nature and culture of their organisations or systems. To this extent, people in systems are not simply victims of environmental forces. The "people-in-systems" perspective recognises that people can become active agents of change within their systems or organisations through interventions based on sound understandings of contemporary happenings in those systems. Such understandings should include a grasp not only of the overt culture of systems but also of the hidden dimensions or "shadow side".

Communication competence represents the third of the perspectives on which adult communication management theory is founded. This perspective has been the subject of considerable scholarly inquiry in interpersonal communication literature. Effectively, the competence perspective relates to both the interpersonal and people-in-systems bases of adult communication management theory, since competence in this sense may refer not only to abilities to relate to other persons but also to the abilities to shape environments so that interpersonal communication is optimised.

Interpersonal Communication

"Communication" is a much abused term, partly because popular writers have tended to restrict its meaning almost exclusively to the exchange of messages, and partly because scholars have broadened its meaning to include anything from direct interpersonal contact to mediated monologue such as radio or television broadcasting. At the heart of all these different conceptions, however, is the conviction and reality that communication is basically a cognitive process. In practice, all people tend to act and communicate on the basis of how they interpret their worlds and their experiences.

Within the literature of contemporary communication theory, the constructivist approach offers a powerful and robust explanation of how interacting individuals interpret and act upon their communication. These scholars defined interpersonal communication as the reciprocal construction of meaning. In their view, people's communication with others is significantly influenced by how they perceive their relationships with those others. According to constructivist theory, individuals create these perceptions and impressions of others and of their relationships with other people, through the application of interpersonal construct systems.

"Constructs" are something like mental building blocks individuals use to develop images of other people. They are traditionally seen as bi-polar adjective pairs like "sincere-insincere" or "expert-inexpert". Constructs may be "physical", such as "tall-short" or "bearded-clean shaven", or they may be "psychological", for instance "friendly-unfriendly" or "trustworthy-untrustworthy".

The constructivists argue that the more psychological interpersonal constructs individuals use in forming impressions or images of others, the more cognitively complex they become. In this sense, cognitive complexity has been traditionally measured by means of the Role Category Questionnaire (RCQ). Over recent years, the intellectual legitimacy and integrity of the cognitive complexity concept has been vigorously challenged. Essentially, critics of constructivist theory have proposed that cognitive complexity is nothing more than loquacity or verbosity. Despite this criticism, no useful alternative to the RCQ measure has to date been proposed.

As is evident, the notion of cognitive complexity is crucial to the rationale of constructivism. People form impressions of other individuals on the basis of the constructs they typically use. Guided by these impressions, people then make "strategic choices" about how to communicate with and act toward others. This process strongly suggests that the accuracy of these impressions and perceptions becomes an important issue. Misperceptions or misinterpretations of others' intentions may lead to unnecessary deterioration or destabilisation of potentially worthwhile interpersonal relationships. This point is particularly relevant to the context of formal learning, where effective learner-facilitator relationships and communication are closely associated with desired learning outcomes.

It has been further suggested that people use their interpersonal construct systems to attribute meaning to the behaviour and communication of others.

Additionally, since attribution theory attempts to explain how people ascribe reasons for the ways in which others communicate and act, the nature and number of constructs individuals use to attribute cause for others' communication assume critical importance.

Based on their interpretations of why certain people act and communicate as they do, individuals develop their own preferred ways of communicating with others. Nevertheless, since interacting persons construct images of each other and of the state of their relationship, their communication is optimal when they share, coordinate, and clarify their perceptions. This kind of reciprocity usually ensures that any misattributions of intent or disposition surface before they become the basis for future communication and behaviour.

Although, in one sense, human communication principles may be regarded as generic, it is difficult to argue against the notion that the systems in which people communicate do have some influence on the nature and quality of that communication. It has been subsequently elaborated and refined, mainly through the introduction of a change management focus.

The essence of the people-in-systems approach is that the design elements of the system-for example the goals of the system, or the structure of the system -have an impact on the quality and amount of communication between people in the system. Implicit in this imperative is the notion that absence of feedback or communication leaves one in a state of uncertainty. As is now well established, the reduction of uncertainty provides one basis for the development of improved communication.

As has been already argued, the communication and behaviour of people can be affected by the nature and structure of the system in which they happen to be situated. The term "system" effectively means more than "organisation", since it refers to anything from a nuclear family to a community. There are all kinds of systems. Schools, hospitals, and prisons are systems. Local sporting clubs, professional societies, and PTA groups are also systems. All these systems differ in their effectiveness and manner in which they operate. In recent times, serious attempts have been made to identify the qualities which distinguish effective from ineffective systems.

For understanding and managing change within systems, the people-in-systems perspective emphasises the need for change agents to recognise the presence of a "shadow side" in any system. The shadow side is typified by happenings which are not sanctioned as or considered to be part of the overt culture of a system. Included here are the hidden agendas, the unwritten rules, the informal norms and practices, and generally, anything which can "mess up" a system. In short, the shadow side is characterised by events that are unpredictable and often undiscussable. The word "arationality" has also been used to refer to the shadow side of systems, since shadow side occurrences cannot be readily explained in terms of logic or the absence of it.

Overall, the people-in-systems perspective consists of two parts or "models". The more recently developed version of Model A is concerned with mapping a system by examining the "current scenario (or story)" and postulating a "preferred scenario (or story)". In this sense, it has a certain strategic quality because it is future-oriented. The scenarios focus noticeably on factors affecting the behaviour and communication of people in their systems. For example, in any scenario one might consider such issues as role clarity, responsibilities and accountabilities, levels of professional relationships, flat or hierarchical management structures, and status and power differentials. It also takes cognisance of the "leverage" people in systems have in order to effect change. Some principles of leverage include time, financial resources, market forces, and current levels of staff competence. Once the degree of leverage has been considered, one is able to develop a strategy to move from the current to the preferred state.

Coincidentally, this model was developed before the more recent move toward understanding the phenomenon of "storytelling" in organisational settings. This concept of "storytelling" refers essentially to the ways in which people construct meanings about other individuals with whom they interact and the systems in which they operate. It has also been suggested that changes in storytelling may lead to changes in systems. Thus, it has been noted that people think of organisations as mansions with many rooms where people engage in conversation to do their work. people will tell stories to make sense of, and to effect change within and outside, that mansion. If we can change the stories that are told and who gets invited to a conversation room to tell stories, then we can change that organisation.

Whilst the interpersonal communication perspective is at the core of the adult communication management framework, the concept of competence has been specifically introduced to address issues of how effectively people in systems communicate with each other. According to Parks, "communicator (or "communicative") competence" has been explained in three different ways. Firstly, it has been understood as the ability of people to maximise the achievement of their goals. Thus, communicator competence "represents the degree to which individuals perceive they have satisfied their goals in a given social situation without jeopardising their ability or opportunity to pursue their other subjectively more important goals". This definition seems to place communicator competence within the framework of thinking and action associated with personal control, a notion at the heart of nearly all conceptualisations of communicator competence.

Communicator competence may alternatively be described in terms of the component abilities or skills which collectively represent the competence domain. One problem with this approach is the difficulty of deciding which skills are the most essential, both from the point of view of present survival and future development. Listening appears to be the component skill most often emphasised. It is closely followed by references to assertiveness, the expression and interpretation of nonverbal cues, conflict resolution and overcoming communication apprehension. As applied to educational settings, "questioning" has become seen, in recent times, as a very important communication skill for teachers.

In addition to considerations of goal achievement and interpersonal skills, a third approach to understanding and developing communicator competence involves the evaluation, by someone like an observer or supervisor, of an individual's communication and actions. The evaluation of communicator competence is usually based on the following criteria: "(1) the ability to formulate and achieve objectives; (2) the ability to collaborate effectively with others i.e. to be interdependent; and (3) the ability to adapt appropriately to situational or environmental variations".

Regardless of which approach one uses to understand and develop communicator competence, there are three important points which need to be kept in mind. Firstly, competence implies more than the possession of "skill". Competence involves a combination of knowledge, skills, attitudes and values which distinguish professionals from technicians. "Competence", in essence, presupposes one's ability to operate at sophisticated levels of reasoning and thinking. This notion is brought out in Peter's claim that the professional's actions and communication are based on "higher-level abstractions".

A second point about the nature of competence is that there are varying degrees of excellence associated with performance of particular professional roles. For example, individuals may be minimally competent, moderately competent, or highly competent. Despite the fact that these gradations are both idiosyncratic and arbitrary, they serve to illustrate the point that competence does not simply equal some ultimate point of excellence. On this basis, it seems reasonable to suggest that the development and refinement of competence is potentially a lifelong process. In theory, adults can manage their communication with others more effectively as a result of systematic and mature reflection on personal and interpersonal experiences.

The final point to be made about communication competence is that there have been very few attempts to apply understandings of communication competence to workplace settings. This has certainly been true of educational workplace settings. The subfield of instructional communication appears to have operated somewhat independently of the subfields of interpersonal or organisational communication. For predictable reasons, the three subfields continue to maintain relatively separate identities.

In summary, the three contributing perspectives which inform adult communication management theory at present, logically integrate in a particular way. The core, represented by the interpersonal communication perspective, is embedded within the people-in-systems conceptual framework. Thus, interpersonal communication or, "the lifeblood of systems", is understood in terms of how system members influence or are influenced by forces shaping particular systems. Finally, competent communicators are those who are able to exercise a measure of control over their social environments. To this extent, their competence may be conceived as a form of leadership which has the potential to bring about personal, interpersonal, and organisational change.

Judging by the increasing interest of postgraduate scholars in adult communication management, it would seem that adult vocational educators see adult communication management theory not simply as a selective pot-pourri of fashionable contemporary theories of human communication. Instead, adult communication management is seen as an appropriate theoretical framework for developing an epistemology of practice. Hopefully, there will be other opportunities for the adult communication management perspective to develop and be refined as a result of constructive and intellectually challenging criticism from contemporary scholars in applied communication theory and research.

Changing Cultural Channels

Australian identity is a product of history and geography. History has contributed an overlay of two centuries of predominantly white European colonisation on land occupied for the previous 40,000 - 50,000 years by Aboriginal people. In more recent times, geography has forced a recognition of Australia as a country located in an Asian context, well placed to be a link between eastern and western nations, and called into question traditional links such as the British connection.

Australia like all nations is a site of contestation between different cultures. It is an arena of transformative practices as a population largely derived from migrants and their offspring attempts to align traditions and cultural practices deriving from their homeland, or some imaginary view of it, with the prevailing conditions of existence here. Any version of national identity and national culture is an invention and involves parallelisms and dualities. Far from being a seamless construct, identity comprises a series of emergent and continually negotiated discourses.

Except in the case of the Aboriginal people, these discourses incorporate reference points drawn from some "home" culture. In Australia, the most notable of these are drawn from Britain: legal systems, educational systems and so on. According to the Australian Bureau of Statistics, the dominant ethnic group in Australia, accounting for around 48% of the population is Anglo-Celtic; 22% are non-Anglo Celtic; while the remaining 30% comprise a mixed Anglo-Celtic and non Anglo-Celtic group deriving from intermarriage.

For the first two hundred years, the Anglo-Celtic group has been dominant, using the fiction of terra nullius to dispossess the Aboriginal people and destroy the fabric of Aboriginal society. In recent times, as the proportion of Anglo-Celtic Australians has diminished, the dominance of this group has been questioned, and this questioning has led to significant movements towards social justice for Aborigines and to an acceptance of multiculturalism as a national policy for all Australians.

Multiculturalism recognises the rights of minority groups to maintain an appropriate cultural identity within the social, political and economic frame of the Australian nation. It underpins national policies such as immigration, equal opportunity, affirmative action and opposition to racism. It is a social and cultural project of nation-building, arguing for continuity between homeland and Australian social context. Multiculturalism is an integrative project, designed to provide equality of opportunity and to lead to greater economic and national cohesion. It is, of course, contested by conservative elements in Australian society, those who have most to lose by any adjustments to the status quo.

Television plays an important role in this process as an agent of popular socialisation. Popular socialisation connotes the evolution of common cultural understandings in relation to such issues as sense of identity, notions of citizenship and the development of ideology, in its broadest sense of knowledge of the world. In his work National Identity, some argues that national identity comprises two related elements: the national political, constituted of the common political and civic conventions involving citizenship and equality before the law, and the national cultural, the core of popular memory, myths, symbols, value systems and significant imagery that are shared by a nation.

Television, along with other forms of cultural production, works at development of the national political and the national cultural at various levels of society. It supports this by acting as a vehicle for their transmission, but it may also challenge and subvert them. It contributes to the construction of the national political through news and current affairs and to the construction of national cultural through drama, "infotainment" and documentary, while sport and other programs may contribute to both or neither.

As a medium-sized nation with English as its major language and situated in both physical and existential terms at the cusp of British and American influence, Australia must rely on a substantial proportion of imported television programs to maintain the operation of its three commercial networks as well as its two government-supported television networks, the Australian Broadcasting Corporation (ABC), and the Special Broadcasting Service (SBS). This differentiates it from both Britain and the USA which have the population to support programming which is predominantly locally produced.

Consequently, Australian television programming is a mix of local and imported, and therefore an intersection point of economic and cultural policies. For this reason, ownership and control of television and other media, and concern about the provision of local content are significant elements on this Australian political agenda. Without a degree of government intervention and regulation, it is conceivable that the production of quality Australian television drama would be severely constrained by the availability of drama produced outside Australia, mainly in the USA, at costs which are a fraction of the cost of mounting comparable Australian productions. While this might be a reasonable situation in strictly economic terms, it is undesirable, even pernicious, in terms of the development of the national cultural elements of Australian identity.

The problems of maintaining programming which contributes to the mainstream of Australian culture are considerable given the economic realities of Australian television. The issue of presenting minority programs in line with the policy of multiculturalism is yet more difficult, since inevitably the audience segments for such programming are small, irrespective of the nature of the minority group. If such a minority group is of non-English speaking background, then special provisions are required to provide such programming.

For example, two such special cases will be considered. They are SBS-TV, a government-funded multicultural television network, and Imparja, a commercial television service owned and operated by Aboriginal people serving a vast but sparsely populated area of central Australia.

SBS TV

The establishment of the Special Broadcasting Service or SBS came from a convergence of cultural and technological circumstances during the 1970s and 1980s. The actual initiative was part of prime minister Malcolm Fraser's policy speech in 1977, and its implementation over the next three years was achieved in the face of considerable opposition. The government even overrode the recommendations of a senate committee that multicultural television should be provided by way of a second ABC channel rather than a separate organisation.

The charter of the SBS called for the provision of television programs "in community languages and English to entertain, inform and educate" both ethnic communities and the broader community, and "to foster the appreciation and development of the cultural diversity of Australian society". Unlike its existing radio services, SBS-TV was planned as a multicultural service, with English subtitles provided for ethnic language programs.

Its programming policies called for around 75% of programs to come from non-English speaking overseas countries. This coupled with severe funding constraints led to considerable innovation in programming. For example, its highly acclaimed news was developed using satellite-delivered VisNews stories not taken up by the ABC or commercial services, supplemented by material from weekly programs provided by overseas government broadcasting services, and by small segments of locally produced news. From the outset, SBS-TV rejected the concept of flow-on audiences, basic to Australian commercial television programming, in favour of audiences who would "visit" the service for specific programs.

At first, programs were confined to Sydney and Melbourne and were broadcast on the VHF band, using channels 0 and 28. With the advent of the AUSSAT satellite in the mid-1980s, the network, now retitled SBS-TV, was established, although it was relocated on the UHF band. This change led to a reduction in homes receiving SBS in Sydney and Melbourne, where the UHF service has still not reached the level of penetration that existed before 1985, since it requires a special antenna and is subject to local interference.

Despite these changes, the fundamental policies of obtaining 75% of programs overseas, and maintaining a 50:50 balance of English and non-English programs were retained. During the early 1980s Greeks, Italians and Yugoslavs were the major ethnic audiences for SBS. In the second half of the 1980s, the emphasis shifted. A greater proportion of program time was dedicated to middle-Eastern and Islamic countries, while Asian language programs were added. With the Australian Bicentenary in 1988, considerable pressure was applied for an increase in Aboriginal programming, with the Aboriginal current affairs program, First in Line going to air in 1989. SBS had earlier pioneered drama about Aborigines with its excellent series Women of the Sun as early as 1982. Some of these shifts are evident in the evolution of SBS identification segments over the decade.

The trend away from ethnicity towards minority interests based on sexual preference, environmental issues and religious affiliations accelerated in the late 1980s. This shift from ethnicity as major emphasis was evident in the changes over time in the format of the news and current affairs programs that contributed substantially to SBS reputation for quality programming. From its inception SBS had aimed at delivery of a "world" news service. This resulted as much from financial constraints as from cultural policy. Analysis of mainstream commercial and ABC news services indicated that they used very few of the overseas news items delivered daily by satellite services such as VisNews, the ABC averaging four and the commercials two to three. This allowed SBS to build a reputation for comprehensive world news coverage by picking up the unused feeds, and supplementing them with low cost magazine-type news features produced weekly by foreign government information services. Often news from as many as twenty overseas countries is featured in SBS daily one-hour news segments. In line with evolutions in its multicultural mission, an increasing proportion of Australian news is used to frame these foreign news items, and in both news and current affairs, overseas events are related where possible to Australian society. News and current affairs are a major priority of SBS, soaking up 30% of the total budget and an enormous 48% of the available budget for locally produced programs.

Shrewd policies for buying foreign language film and drama also allowed SBS to maximise its sparse resources.

Since mainstream commercial TV programs only English language material, SBS has been able to purchase high quality foreign material at relatively low prices. Most of this foreign language material is subtitled by the SBS, an operation of extremely high quality. "Quality" has been a keystone of SBS programming from the start. In part this was due to a philosophical principle that an ethnic broadcast service could not afford to be viewed as second-rate, in part to a pre-emptive strategy of downgrading ratings as a measure of performance. The quality argument also served as some defence against moral and political censorship, though both would impact upon SBS from time to time.

In terms of audience policies, SBS did not practice the "follow through" approach to audiences practised by the commercials. Rather it pursued a "narrowcast" approach of audience segmentation, with its major targets being specific ethnic or language groups, together with cosmopolitan Australians of other groups. The demographics indicate that this policy has been successful. Over 40% of the SBS audience were born outside Australia and 23% of its audience belong to managerial/professional households. SBS-TV ratings are low, though SBS surveys indicate that some three million Australians view it each week.

The future for the SBS depends upon a number of variables. A new charter allows the SBS to sell commercial time as well as sponsorship, which may provide additional economic stability and possibly additional funds for production. The increased reach of SBS has diminished its proportion of ethnic audience, and this may decline further as immigration declines, while the traditional ethnic groups may be affected by increased Asian migration. SBS programming is vulnerable to political events, both in Australia and overseas as evidenced by the replacement of the Croatian anchor of Vox Populi with an Aborigine following the eruption of ethnic conflict in Eastern Europe.

SBS is also likely to be troubled by its success in developing audiences for world news and foreign-language films when Pay-TV is eventually established.

On the positive side, the continuing movement away from ethnicity towards cultural diversity should broaden the base of audience support for SBS. The nature and diversity of programming coupled with cost effectiveness in terms of output per employee and unit cost of programming suggest that it should remain viable in its specialist niche.

In addition, one might argue that SBS-TV has performed a useful function in providing a model for mainstream Australian televised in meeting the challenges implicit in cultural diversity. These include news protocols for treating cultural pluralism, representation of ethnic identities in non-stereotypical ways in drama and advertising, and incorporation of various multicultural elements into the development of a national cultural appropriate to a poly-ethnic, multilingual society .

Imparja

Like SBS, Imparja was established in the face of considerable opposition. When the Australian Broadcasting Tribunal called applications for Remote Commercial Television Service (RCTS), the Central Australian Aboriginal Media Association (CAAMA) was an applicant. It based its application upon a claim that 38% of the potential audience were Aborigines, and that a majority of the surviving Aboriginal language groups in Australia, some 22 in all with three or four dominant, were found in this region.

The other potential licensee was the Capricornia group based on existing television interests in Darwin's NTD-8. The tribunal process was protracted, but Imparja, the group sponsored by CAAMA, was finally successful, though not without surviving an appeal by the Capricornia group and the Northern Territory government. The approval for Imparja came in April 1987, and operations commenced shortly afterwards in January 1988.

The problems facing Imparja were complex. Just as the public debates about SBS revolved around the rights of minority groups to representation, the politics of ethnicity and questions of social integration and cultural maintenance, so similar questions surrounded the operations of Imparja. They were further complicated by the role of Aboriginal law, knowledge based on oral traditions and other intellectual property jealously guarded by tribal custodians. Aboriginal culture encompasses a mythology, or perhaps more properly a cosmology, which is manifest in stories, songs, dance and graphic design, and which was in the past communicated along traditional geographic song-lines and story-lines.

Consequently, Aboriginal people could see analogies between this traditional information-sharing and the communication lines opened up by satellite technology. There were, of course, problems caused by the arcane nature of some of this information, as well as by challenges to the traditional roles of tribal elders resulting from the greater English proficiency of younger Aborigines, and by prohibitions and restrictions upon the use of images and even of names, particularly where dead people were involved.

However, with a grant from the federal government and additional if reluctant funding from the Northern Territory government who had agreed to buy substantial time from the new television station when it was thought the Darwin group would be successful, Imparja commenced operations as a commercial television station serving some thirty remote communities.

Particular Aboriginal programming on Imparja is embedded within regular services based upon mainstream programs. Imparja Television as the owner of the television licence operates the television station in Alice Springs while CAAMA Productions specialises in programs treating Aboriginal topics, some of which go to air on Imparja. Both are part of the same group of companies, which are owned by Aboriginal interests.

Since Imparja is a commercial operation, its programming must attract sponsorship, and currently its operating costs exceed its government grant of A$2 million by around A$700,000. Consequently only around 2% of Imparja's programming is Aboriginal, notably the news program Urrpeye and the magazine-style program Nganampa, which were intended for broadcast in three Aboriginal languages with English subtitles. The cost of producing these Aboriginal language programs is, however, prohibitively high. As yet, Aboriginalisation of the management of Imparja and of its creative staff has been limited.

In the Aboriginal communities of Yuendumu in the Northern Territory and Ernabella in South Australia, a form of Aboriginal television has developed. Using equipment provided by the Australian government under its Broadcasting for Remote Aboriginal Communities Scheme (BRACS), local Aboriginal media groups are producing programs which are interpolated in the programs received from the satellite. In this context, the production, distribution and financing of these local programs is under Aboriginal control.

The programs are often educational, adapting the format of mainstream children's programs for local conditions and featuring local people and language. Some others might be properly termed cultural maintenance, as they record traditional songs and dance for dissemination to Aborigines who are ignorant of them. Yet others record secret ceremonies and are consequently not available for general viewing.

While Imparja indicates one way television can contribute to the incorporation of Aboriginal culture within the national cultural, it also shows problems of Aboriginalisation of programming and personnel in the context of a commercial broadcast service. Ernabella and Yuendumu provide an example of Aboriginal control of incoming television programs, at least in part, and of attempts to inscribe culturally appropriate forms within mainstream television programming.

Imparja and SBS-TV represent two approaches to the problem of minority groups contributing to the national cultural through access to television. SBS-TV has evolved from a principal focus on ethnic minorities to a more general interpretation of multiculturalism based on a diversity of minority interests. By any standard, SBS- TV should be judged as successful in development of national cultural elements.

Imparja, on the other hand, clearly reflects the tensions operating in attempting to reconcile commercial operations with the representation of a particular cultural group which has little economic resource. Perhaps a model for Aboriginal television based along lines similar to SBS, allowing for a broadcast service across Northern Australia with provision for inclusion of special interest Aboriginal and Torres Strait Island insert programs, or utilising common dialects such as Kriol, might constitute a more viable indigenous television scheme.

SBS-TV and Imparja comprise uniquely Australian attempts to allow indigenous and other minorities to find representation on Australian television screens, and in this way to allow incorporation of Aboriginal and other minoritarian interests and images within the national cultural and the national political of the Australian nation. They are significant attempts to contribute to a genuinely multicultural Australia.

Impact of Communication and Information Technologies in the Home

The body of theory and research encompassed by the label, "the domestic paradigm", has been published in a series of works through which its evolution can be traced. Insofar as there is a single term with which these researchers do refer to their own work, it would be "ethnographic".

This term, borrowed from anthropology but given a cultural studies twist, is intended to signify the qualitative empirical observation of everyday life in family households which characterizes the methodology of these researchers: Audiences are not simply or only watchers of television or listeners to radio: they are members of families, households, communities and nations; they are gendered, aged and members of social classes; they are skilled and unskilled, educated and uneducated; and they watch television while doing other things and in competition with other things, at times and in places, alone and with others, in ways that mark their activity as powerfully mediated by the social, economic, political and technological systems and structures of everyday life.

The domestic paradigm makes what is perhaps its most distinctive theoretical contribution in the linkage it asserts between the micro world of the household and the macro context of institutional structure, conceived at both levels in terms of space and time. At the micro level, the use of television in the home is the entry point for its analysis of how all communication and information technologies (CITs) are related to the organization of domestic space and to the temporal routines and social rituals and relations in the household.

The macro aspect is even more striking for its bold conception which draws together various observations about how communications media have rationalized the use of both "calendrical" and "quotidian" time in households across the space of the nation. The advent of "mass" media has given rise to the social construction of citizenship and a sense of membership of the nation, binding individuals in their households into what Benedict Anderson calls the "imagined community" of the nation.

The domestic paradigm researchers formulate this insight in these terms: "Television has to be seen as embedded within a technical and consumer culture that is both domestic and national, a culture that is at once both private and public".

This quotation raises two further aspects of the theoretical underpinnings of the domestic paradigm: its conception of the household and the special place which television occupies within its scheme. They speak of the "moral economy" of the household, by which is meant the cultural means by which a household asserts its sense of itself and its place in the world, "what makes a house a home". Household members use CITs to establish boundaries within and around the household, that is, assert their collective and individual statuses and identities through their styles of consumption and social use of CITs, relative to time and space as well as to the moral economy.

The final conceptual component of the domestic paradigm which deserves mention here is the "double articulation thesis" which they apply to television, which provides the rationale for taking television as the model for the analysis of all CITs. In essence, the double articulation thesis is that television is not just a transmitter of meaningful message content, that is of information, entertainment and advertisements, but it is also meaningful in itself. In the domestic paradigm, television's meaning as an object is seen to be analogous to the meaning of its messages.

The consumption of both objects and messages is a process of constructing meanings, but not just any meanings: "one is not able to treat the individual viewer as if he or she were a free or rational consumer in a cultural supermarket". One chooses goods or meanings from what others make available, and in terms of one's given cultural and material resources.

The design and implementation of the actual research carried out under the domestic paradigm, as well as raise some limitations which invite other modes of investigation. Silverstone acknowledges that the domestic paradigm is "a reformulation of the classic enquiry into the power of the media". However, it is also important to see how far there has been an expansion of scope beyond the particular medium of television to include other CITs, notably the telephone and the computer, in addition to new television-based technologies as the VCR. To this extent, the theoretical development and the methodological lessons gained from decades of television studies might be applied to advance research into the social significance of technologies which are much newer or which have been neglected in the past, the telephone in particular.

Because television has been "constructed as domestic", Silverstone calls it the household's "leading object". However, he recognizes that although each domestic CIT has its own intrinsic mode of use and significance, television should not now be studied in isolation, but in the context of the "domestic socio-technical system" as a whole, which includes telecommunications, audio reproduction (CD, tape players and radios) and photovisual "objects" (still and video cameras) as well as the household's television set(s) and attendant remote control and VCR.

It follows that audiences should not be studied in isolation either, least of all in the traditional mould as broadcast audiences. The perception that the television screen has become the medium of successive new forms of domestic CIT hardware (the VCR), software (videogames) and service (teletext, subscription TV) is a commonplace rather than a particular insight of the domestic paradigm.

However, what the domestic paradigm does offer in the context of such new technologies is a theoretical rationale in which to conceptualize their social impact, and closely related empirical methods with which to implement actual research, not so much on the "social effects of television", as on the use and significance of the whole socio-technical system or "techno- culture" of the household.

At this point we are ready to look more closely at the actual implementation of this British research in its most recent phase. The unit of investigation which was taken was not the household in general, but that of the nuclear family, which, in Britain as in Australia, is still the most common form of household as well as the one which occupies a central ideological position as the preferred social ideal. For the practical and investigative purposes of the Brunel project the twenty families selected were affluent enough to own three out of four "core" CITs (television, telephone, computer and video), had school-age children, spoke English and were mainly white.

The first stage of the study used a time-use diary as well as "participant observation" and a family interview. However, the participant observation method was not found to be adequate to the research questions, and when the (woman) field researcher left the study, the research on the remaining sixteen families was carried out with a new design, and over periods of up to ten months. This design was composed of a "raft" of several methods of data generation, so that data derived from one method could be triangulated against others.

It is evident that, on the basis of experience in the first phase, the research made a shift away from a fairly open-ended conception of ethnography as a form of participant observation, and towards a series of research tools which not only were tailored to the project's quite specific purposes, but also served as a means of checking and comparing one kind of data against another. This adaptation has no doubt produced a more rigorous and structured form of ethnography. As well, they claim, it has built in a reflexive factor, both for the researchers and the researched. To a great extent, this more purpose-built yet malleable application of ethnographic method answers various reservations which have been expressed about it.

Some other shifts are also apparent. Earlier work under this paradigm was motivated by a concern with the social distribution of cultural competence, that is, with the socially structured access to the "codes" of cultural knowledge which audiences brought to bear in interpreting media messages, conceived very much in class terms. Subsequent research in this respect shifted attention towards gender.

In the Brunel phase, this has been accompanied by a parallel move which has reprioritized the whole question of media interpretations by audiences, apparent at the level of research design in the diminished position which inquiries into media use have within the raft of methods. What has been lost in terms of understanding the broader class-based distribution of cultural competence in the society at large, however, is compensated by a more intensive approach to social reproduction as it is manifested in the "gendering" of CITs by the domestic division of labour: for example, the question of who knows how to use which technology, how the skills and knowledge are learned, and for what purposes they are applied.

However, a final observation on how the domestic paradigm has developed in the course of being applied in research has to do with the implications which qualitative, reflexive, ethnographic research can have for the number of households which can be studied and reported on in this manner, and for their representativeness.

Nevertheless, if this method is to gain credibility amongst policymakers and others who have more pragmatic expectations of research findings, and who are schooled in more orthodox social science procedures, there needs to be some built-in measure through which a judgement can be made about the social location of the households being studied. This is not to demand that the households be "typical" in some way, but rather, to ensure that they can be identified within a set of meaningful sociological indicators.

It was with this concern about social location in mind that a two-phase research design was devised in the study reported here. The first phase sought to select households suitable for ethnographic investigation in the second phase, but did so on the basis of quantitative information elicited about each household's socioeconomic and cultural characteristics, and their gross patterns of CIT ownership and use.

The research was conceived as an exploratory study towards a much broader and long-term project which would investigate a range of social factors in the use of CITs, both within and between different types of nuclear family household in suburban Australia. The project hypothesises that such households are "interpretive communities" which each have their certain skills, cultural codes and attitudes relevant to CIT use, but also that these are determined by the social location of the household within the unequal patterns in which these skills, codes and attitudes are distributed through the society. Furthermore, just as differences between families in socioeconomic status, ethnolinguistic origin and education are identified as the decisive variables to be investigated in such social distribution, it is also hypothesised that within families there will be found differences in patterns of use and attitudes towards CITs determined by gender and age.

While it was considered desirable that there be a broad comparative alignment of this project with the Brunel work which inspired it, the pilot study at least has had to make adaptations of a practical nature. Thus, unlike the Brunel study's focus on families with school-age children, some families with adult children and others with pre-school children were included in the pilot study under report here.

Again, while the Brunel study required families to possess three out of four "core" CITs, a priori this one did not, although most families in the sample turned out to "qualify" in this respect. As to linguistic and ethnic homogeneity, quite a different process and purpose applied than in the Brunel work, in that families of non-English speaking background (NESB) were not excluded. However, because NESB families tended to be uncertain and suspicious towards the research, they rendered a low rate of return. Thus, 85% of the sample achieved were from English-speaking households.

The use of a questionnaire as a research instrument in this study marks a fundamental difference from the Brunel team's triangulated raft of methods. The questionnaire was chosen as a means of rapidly eliciting descriptive but quantifiable data from a workable sample of families across a selected suburban region, given the limitations of how many families could have been interviewed and for how long by a single researcher, working unaided in a short time-frame. In addition to the collection of broad descriptive data for a reasonable number of households, the questionnaire approach was selected with the intention of identifying families who would be eligible and willing to engage themselves in an interview with the researcher in the ethnographic second phase.

Another important variation from the Brunel approach was the intention that the families in the sample would be, if not "representative" of, at least selected from, a substantial and identifiable social stratum of suburban Melbourne. Thus, a two-stage sampling procedure was applied in which five suburbs were chosen across the breadth and depth of the western region of Melbourne. The study thus sought to select families in the broad socioeconomic zone between the "middle" and working class, or the "lower-middle" and "upper-working" categories, if these terms have any objective meaning.

Of the 45 households which answered the question on gross family income, the majority were receiving annual family incomes in a range which compared to the 53% of all Australian households which were in the medium income category in the 1986 Census. In terms of occupation, most households had just one major breadwinner. The Australian Standard Classification of Occupations (ASCO) system is based on type of work rather than socioeconomic status, but it is reasonable to infer from this distribution that the profile of the sample is quite broad in that regard, rather more towards the "middle class" than received stereotypes of the western suburbs would suggest. Thus, in this and other respects, the sampled households were fairly within the social stratum which the study had sought.

In terms of the social use of space and time within the home, it can be hypothesised from this sample that video is the most versatile domestic technology, instrumental to the moral economy of the household in that it allows the family members to accommodate each other's different demands upon the "leading object" of the television. However, the presence of television sets in the private space of the bedroom in some homes might indicate that they have a more individualised and less family-oriented moral economy. In this way, the questionnaire results are suggestive for lines of investigation to be taken in the subsequent ethnographic investigation. Radio appears to be a medium adapted to both family and individual use.

On questions of CIT use, the households reported an average of 6.7 hours for how long the television was on each day, and 2.6 for radio. These figures need to be compared to the responses to questions put to individual members of the household, asking them how long they actually sat down and watched television or listened to the radio. Parents watched an average of 3.05 hours and children 3.3

hours of television, less than half the time the set is on. For radio, parents at least were more attentive: the figures were 2.0 and 1.0 respectively. More than half of the households with computers reported that they were mainly used for children's games, less than a quarter for school work. The children estimated that they used the computers for an average of one hour per week.

In an attempt to gain some quantitative sense of the social boundaries and rituals which families develop around their CITs, households were asked about the rules governing the children's television watching. Bearing in mind that almost half these families have at least one child 18 or over, it is not surprising that a minority of households, just over a third in fact, said they thought they had "strict rules". However, when this response was checked against the responses of individual children, an even smaller proportion of children thought so.

Ethnographic observation should be able to reveal the degree to which this difference is one of perception or actual practice. Families were also asked if they usually ate their meals together, and 85% of them said they did, but in a clear majority of cases, it was with the television on in the same room. It would appear that this practice is one form in which a major public medium of communication commonly intersects with a private domestic ritual, but again, ethnographic observation is needed to see just how it is negotiated in different households.

In order to see if the recession was having much impact upon CIT expenditure, respondents were asked if they had been forced to have the phone disconnected. Only two replied that they had, and another two said that they had sold their video. There were also questions asked to gauge expenditure on certain entertainment goods, namely videotapes and audiotapes or compact discs. Households with video spent an average of $4 per week on hiring tapes - one per week in effect. Asked about cassettes and CDs, just over 25% of the children advised they had bought some in the previous year, most saying less than five.

One other media expenditure item was more notional: how much the household would be prepared to spend on pay-TV, as a weekly average. At a time when the future structure and scope of broadcast regulation in Australia was in play, it was instructive to discover the solid popular support, at least amongst this sample of families, in favour of the principle of transmission quotas for Australian programs. Amongst parents, 95% affirmed their agreement with a summary statement of this principle, while 100 out of the 137 children, or 73%, also agreed.

Furthermore, over 70% of parents and an only slightly smaller percentage of children named Australian programs amongst their favourites, and when asked if they liked them because they were Australian or because they were "good programs", from 85% to 100% of those respondents in each category answered the latter. Several made a point by ticking both boxes: questionnaires are not necessarily as restrictive as they are reputed to be.

Finally, there was the crucial question intended to enable the selection of interviewee families for the second, "ethnographic" stage of the project: would the family be willing to talk to the researcher at length about all these things? Of the 61 questionnaire families, only four said that they would. One of these was not appropriate, being a couple with a nine-month old baby, and when the other three were approached by letter with a view to making an appointment, only one responded.

The main point to be made in conclusion is that although the clustered sampling and administration of the household questionnaire was designed principally as a means of selecting families for ethnographic interview and of generating supporting descriptive data, that data has gone beyond expectations in the degree of its representativenes and in the detail of patterns of CIT ownership and use it delineates. In regard to family size and type, income and housing, the sample can be taken as representative of middle Australia, or at least, the urban, English-speaking sector of it, which is still a majority of the population.

It should also be said that in addition to the gross ownership and use data, the questionnaire has been able to produce information on attitudes to current policy issues; to document certain aspects of CIT-related behaviour, such as the difference between the hours spent attending to television and radio, and the hours the sets are on; and even to reveal attitudinal differences in how family members relate to CITs, seen in the difference between parents and children on the question of strict rules.

Clearly, it is necessary to use means other than doorstepping to find families willing to be intensively interviewed in the manner which the ethnographic domestic paradigm requires. In this regard, the strategy used in the Brunel study of approaching prospective families through schools would seem to be a more effective and accessible option. It lends the research a legitimacy which a doorstep approach could never expect to achieve. The subsequent interview can then draw out the complexities of behaviour and attitudes which a questionnaire can only indicate in relatively crude categories.

This is to raise the prospect of how the triangulation of ethnographic interviews with more widely-gathered questionnaire data might bring the domestic paradigm to a new stage, one in which it is possible to single out particular social factors for investigation. This would not be done in the sense or spirit in which positivist science isolates dependent and independent variables, runs control groups and tests specific hypotheses. That entire mode of investigation is alien and inappropriate to what is being suggested here. Rather, the prospect arises for the exploration of differences in CIT use between families defined by selected contrasting social characteristics.

Research could look for patterns of difference associated with language used at home between families in the same neighbourhood and of similar structure and socioeconomic status. Researchers could select an area in which there was known to be a large number of speakers of a certain language, say, Spanish. Household questionnaires could then be administered to selected clusters of homes, while families for interview were recruited through the local school. Such a design could yield both extensive, quantitative and intensive, qualitative data of a comparative nature on both English-speaking and Spanish-speaking families. It is not difficult to imagine how other such contrasts could be set up: high-income versus low-income; well-educated versus poorly-educated; younger versus older families; even at a later stage, nuclear versus other family types. A similar prospect exists for the investigation of not just CIT use in general, but of particular technologies. As well as their considerable interest for academic social scientists, the findings from such research would be valuable to actual and potential service providers, and also bear significant social and communication policy implications.

9

Media and Social Variables

Concept of Meaning-making

The concept of meaning-making in the media environment lends itself to naturalistic media inquiries. Such inquiries claim to examine the social conditions in which media content gets encountered, interpreted, and acted upon. Central to media ethnographies are the assumptions that media content can be decoded in numerous ways and that the terms of these decodings can be traced to meaning-making processes through which social actors construct their everyday conditions.

Some studies recently offered an analysis of a particular variety of media ethnographies that termed "accommodation" approaches. That accommodation media ethnographers ignore central issues of textual, historical, and material influences on audience interactions with the media. These contentions are summarized in the premise that accommodation approaches emphasize social situations at the expense of central meanings in media content, thus treating social actors as free-floating, ahistorical interpretive agents.

At the heart of these contentions appears to be the assumption that the interpretivist paradigm is incapable of addressing significant historical, political, and other social variables. Carragee's analysis, however, does not make direct contact with the theoretical bases it attempts to critique. It relies, instead, on second-hand accounts of various philosophers of science whose social science positions were critiqued equally by various interpretivist philosophers.

More direct examinations of the interpretivist bases critiques suggests that the interpretivist position clearly makes provisions for addressing matters of history, social power, etc. Recent publications have, nevertheless, reiterated contentions, thus characterizing the nature and role of social situations in accommodation ethnographies in questionable ways. On the other hand, practitioners of accommodation media ethnographies have also missed the opportunity to direct their attention to fundamental theoretical matters regarding social situations.

Although various accommodation media ethnographers have described and aptly illustrated principles about social situations, they have not advanced the theoretical rationales that justify why social situations should be given such importance. The result has been the lack of a sensible working base from which to respond to recent criticisms. In an effort to move these matters in a more positive direction, the present analysis presents a set of propositions about social situations on which accommodation media approaches are often based. It supports these propositions by linking them to the historic scholarship from which accommodation premises are often derived. This historic scholarship indicates how and why accommodation media approaches are theoretically equipped to address significant issues of social power, history, etc. In addition, these sources indicate why social situations are given the kind of emphasis they receive in accommodation media literature.

The manner by which social situations are theoretically defined and studied is unique in accommodation media approaches. The meanings produced for these social behaviors are said to provide at least a portion of the meanings audiences use while attending to media content.

Any meanings offered by media content get mingled with these other meanings. The resulting interplay of meanings produces options for the kinds of meanings audiences can use to further direct their activities. Audiences can perpetuate, modify, change, or replace meanings for their content, their activities, or both. These options give rise to indeterminacies in meaning that audiences attempt to manage.

Such management efforts are assumed to result in various kinds of media-related social behaviors that (1) direct other social activities, (2) get directed by other social activities, or (3) take place concurrently with other social activities. Eating dinner could determine how one watches television; watching television could determine how one eats dinner; or watching television and eating dinner could merge into a single line of action that requires particular forms of behavior and resources. Accommodation media ethnographies reflect efforts to identify these management efforts and the consequences they bring about in audience members' lives.

The uniqueness of this "behavior text" concept is best seen by comparing accommodation media approaches to other kinds of media research. Anderson and Meyer's typology classifies media research as either (1) traditional, (2) cultural interpretive, or (3) accommodation interpretive.

Traditional media is characterized as locating the cause of media effects in media content and, more specifically, in the manner by which this content is constructed and codified. Such research presumes that the effects of content appear in individual behavior that results from exposure to content and its meaning codes. Media-related behaviors are assumed to be mere sites of exposure with no further meaning or import.

In contrast, accommodation media approaches see both media-related and subsequent behaviors as representing larger, collective patterns of social interaction. Any observed individual behavior-media-related or otherwise-is interpreted to be a sign of participation in some larger, collective, and thematic action. It is this larger pattern of collective action that is said to be the source of media effects.

The larger pattern is assumed to be produced through the coordinated efforts of social actors who interpret their own and others' behaviors in order to carry out various lines of action. The meanings produced through this larger pattern of action will determine what meanings will be attended to and used in any given moment of audience behavior. Rather than study the relationship between individual behaviors and media content, then, accommodation approaches study the ways in which media content gets accommodated to these larger action patterns.

Content is seen as being coded with several levels of possible meanings. Social forces (e.g., government, advertising, media industries) participate at macroscopic levels of meaning production to infuse content with meanings that reflect the broader interests of these power groups. Media audiences, in turn, are viewed as being responsive both to those interests and to those meanings. Such responses can range from proactive to reactive forms of behavior. This form of research has, thus, been championed for granting media audiences with the capacity to construct their own terms of "reality".

Cultural studies have, however, also been criticized for failing to fully examine the nature by which these audience "realities" get constructed with or for media content. Here, the contention is that social situations play a necessary and perhaps central role in meaning construction alongside media content and macroscopic forces. Indeed, accommodation media approaches contend that social situations constitute a meeting ground between the microscopic levels of content and the macroscopic levels of social institutions, history, politics, etc.

Social situations are those spheres of audience activity where matters of culture, belief, etc. manifest themselves in concrete forms of human action. In social situations, media audiences are assumed to bring their social behaviors into being through on-the-spot interpretations and performances of social forms of action. On the macroscopic side, these forms of action are found in historically, politically, and institutionally perpetuated types of social behaviors. Social actors are necessarily constrained by having to choose from a menu of socially provided options for how to proceed with the matter of acting out and continuing daily life. They can behave only with forms of action that others provide.

On the microscopic side, media content and all of its characteristics (symbols, sounds, images, etc.) provide some of the resource options by which social actors can continue to construct their behaviors and-in turn-their daily situations. Content provides such resources both by suggesting courses of action and by being used in potentially unforeseeable ways to produce courses of action. Here, audiences might still respond to potential levels of meaning that are coded into media content.

They can, however, also attend to content in ways that make sense more for the situations in which they are acting than for any meanings suggested by content. Accommodation approaches, therefore, hold that media audiences always produce meanings for their social behaviors and situations along with meanings for media content. Microscopic and macroscopic levels of meaning thus get managed through the management of the meanings for social forms of behavior. The means by which audiences manage these meaning productions, however, may be highly unpredictable.

By taking this view, accommodation media approaches significantly alter many cultural media studies attempts to reconcile microscopic and macroscopic levels of meaning. Accommodation approaches replace the ideas of "infused meaning" (e.g., in content) and "social forces" (i.e., coerced meanings) with the concept of "performed meaning."

Meaning-whether it be for content, social behavior, or institutions-is encountered as indeterminate and in need of management. Whatever management takes place at a local level determines at a given time and place just how content and institutional directives are responded to or brought into play. In relation to both traditional and cultural media studies, then, accommodation media approaches take a unique approach to social situations. They see the study of social situations as the key to understanding the import of media content and the management of social expectations. Studying the means by which audiences go about producing and managing meanings for their social behaviors is assumed to provide vital information about how audiences use media content to construct their social realities.

The overall case that theoretically justifies the accommodation position and its relationship to other forms of media research is beyond the scope of the present analysis. Some work has already been done to articulate the microscopic levels of analysis needed in accommodation media ethnographies; that is, to identify the manner by which audiences are able to work with various content codes.

The work limits itself to the analysis of macroscopic variables and their relationship to audiences' social situations. Where necessary, the work makes general reference to the nature of media content; however, the reader is directed to these other sources to more fully understand how accommodation media approaches characterize media content. Broader explications of how social situations provide management of microscopic and macroscopic levels of meaning will still be in order.

The theoretical premises that direct accommodation views of social situations indicate that significant matters of history and social power are inseparable from these social situations. For convenience, the theoretical justifications for these views are organized here into five interpretivist principles about social behavior, social situations, and media studies:

— Media-related behaviors are social acts for which social actors produce meanings.
— Media-related behaviors get different meanings through forms of social interaction (i.e., social action routines).
— The meanings produced in constellations of media-related and other social acts direct decodings for media content.
— Historic social constraints limit the meanings that can be produced for constellations of media-related and other social acts and, hence, limit decodings for content.
— Historic social constraints and, hence, the terms for decoding media content, can nevertheless be modified through reflexive reconstructions of social routines.

1. Media-related behaviors are social acts for which social actors produce meanings.

Interpretivist scholars view behavior as the foundation of meaning. This view originated in the assumption that the phenomenal world changes as do the perspectives of the actors who inhabit and move within that world. Actors must develop methods by which to render stability out of flux.

The fluctuating phenomenal world can be experienced with stability only if actors enter into repeatable and stable relationships with that world through particular and repeatable lines of action. Lines of action provide a set of fundamental experiences by which the features of the phenomenal world can be regularly selected, attended to, fashioned, and interpreted as "objects," and they thus bring into being a stable "world" about which to produce knowledge. Such meaning production depends, of course, upon how the properties of the phenomenal world lend themselves to, or can be incorporated into, the actions, although there is always the possibility of treating the phenomenal world in imaginary ways.

It must be possible to differentiate, identify, and perform lines of action in certain ways in order to produce and reproduce them. Lines of action, then, must also become "objects" with some denotative meaning that constitutes them as social acts or signs of something being done. They must, in other words, be codable and decodable by being given certain physical forms.

The need to encode lines of action as social acts thus also constitutes the performers of these acts as social actors. In the accommodation philosophy, media-related behaviors (watching television, etc.) are held to constitute particular social acts. By virtue of their being recognized as types of behavior-both by social actors and media researchers-such activities must have some recognizable form that distinguishes them from other kinds of activities. To "watch TV," then, is to enter into a socially understandable form of behavior that can be produced and reproduced with recognizable forms and features.

As social acts, media-related behaviors establish a set of preliminary conditions by which media content might be encountered and decoded. Through the lines of behavior that constitute the act, a media-related behavior brings social actors into potentially stable and repeatable relationships with media content. Here, media content is seen as another facet of the phenomenal world that is subject to change, perhaps even through its own characteristics (e.g., the flow of televised images) or through the changing perspectives of social actors. By being converted into signifying lines of action, however, media-related behaviors provide at least an initial form of relating to content where such changes can be brought under control.

2. Media-related behaviors get different meanings through forms of social interaction (i.e., social action routines)

Because social acts get treated as signs, they are subject to certain characteristics of sign systems. Principally, in the interpretivist position, social acts get their meanings in interaction, wherein such signs get configured in sensible (i.e., syntactical) ways, much as words get sensibly configured to produce sentences. Within different configurations, the same social act can be produced, interpreted, and responded to with a number of possible meanings. Interaction is deemed necessary for regulating the meaning possibilities of all signs and sign systems, including social acts. All signs are seen as giving rise to indeterminacies that must be managed. Such indeterminacies arise through webs of social appropriations, uses, alterations, etc. Interaction provides a framework by which social actors can produce and monitor a limited range of meaning possibilities so as to gain control over these indeterminacies.

Special forms of interaction are needed by which social actors can collectively manage the meaning indeterminacies of social acts. Here, the governing form of interaction is the social action routine. The routine is a pattern for possible interaction that emerges as a single line of coordinated and configured social acts. This line of joint action is considered thematic (e.g., giving a dinner party, holding a meeting, conducting a class) and serves as a reference point to which the actors can turn for guidance in producing, coding, and organizing their social acts.

Within these forms of interaction, social actors will collectively produce and regulate various meanings that can be used to produce, monitor, and direct the collective social behavior. The range of meanings they produce for the routine and its social acts limits or "frames" the meanings that can or cannot be produced by the participants at any given moment. All other meanings produced in a routine must be sensibly managed in such a way that the meanings for the routine can be sustained or at least managed in the face of change. What social acts signify are, thus, the central source of meanings with which social actors work in any routine. These meanings take priority, for they maintain the stability of the situation; without them the social actors would lose their bearings.

The meanings of media-related behaviors will, likewise, emerge through the ways they get performed, organized, and integrated into an overall tapestry of meanings that get produced for a range of social behaviors. This tapestry is directed in and through forms of interaction that sensibly incorporate all local social acts within an overall line of collective action.

Any media-related behavior, as such, implicates at least two social actors working together in guided ways to produce and direct a set of meanings for the activity at hand. For social actors, the problem becomes one of how to sensibly accommodate media-related behaviors with other social acts. In and of themselves, media-related behaviors carry no prescriptions that dictate their significance at any given time. Meanings must be produced, sustained, and directed that allow media-related activities to emerge, continue, be abandoned, be returned to, etc. What it means to "watch TV," then, depends upon what else is going on in a particular routine.

Indeed, it may be that some social acts or whole routines get constituted as "media-related" by virtue of incorporating forms of media, their content, or their manners of attendance. "Eating dinner," for example, might be deemed a particular social routine that gets constituted by including television as a source of conversational topics. Such routines would not necessarily consist of separate, competing, or even concurrent lines of activity but could instead constitute a single line of social action. The centrality of either the media or their manners of attendance within such activity frameworks might, then, vary within a routine or from routine to routine.

3. The meanings produced in constellations of media-related and other social acts direct decodings for media content

The range of meanings that might get produced in the course of a routine provide an overall context of meanings that orients the actors to interpret themselves and their surroundings in certain ways. This range of meanings; however, is always indeterminate. The overall direction of action could shift at any moment, and new meanings may have to be produced or old ones altered in order to sustain the flow of action.

Because the routine emerges as the behaviors get produced, the actors have to continue to monitor, supervise, and direct their own and others' social acts on an ongoing basis. What gets understood, and how it gets understood, is thus dependent on the contingencies of localized action performances and the way(s) in which actors collectively produce and control meanings so as to make those circumstances possible.

The local contingencies of the action routine (available resources, the particular constellation of actors present, the action themes being enacted, etc.) may push social actors to override or redefine some facet of the material or conceptual world-including signs and sign systems-in order to accomplish the social action requirements at hand.

Anything and anyone that gets encountered within the production of a routine will, therefore, have to be understood and managed in terms of the meanings needed to maintain and direct the routine.

In this respect, to decode media content is to use the meanings of social action as a set of terms for attending to content. Such meanings for content must be produced along with the meanings produced for every other facet of the social situation. All people, objects, actions, ideas, etc. that get factored into social routines must be interpreted and managed in sensible ways, and content is part of this meaning- making fabric. Sometimes content may take a central position, and at other times it may take a necessary secondary or tertiary position.

Across a variety of social routines and media-related forms of interaction, the symbolic and nonsymbolic properties of the same media content may have to bend, be bent, or be fragmented to make everyday life work. This view of decoding does not, however, exclude the possibility that some intended or desired meanings might be sought in media content. Decoding content through any of its (possible) signifying characteristics may well be a type of social activity that finds its way (perhaps centrally) in various routines (e.g., a film class). This type of social activity, however, might be only one of many and might be mingled with other social activities and their meaning contexts.

4. Historic social constraints limit the meanings that can be produced for constellations of media-related and other social acts and, hence, limit decodings for content

Many interpretivist scholars recognize the historic, political, and institutional nature of social forms of action. In at least four ways, social interaction constrains the ways social actors might encounter, experience, and act upon social reality. First, social forms of action reflect cultural and institutional prescriptions. Social actors go to great lengths to ensure the maintenance of their locally produced meanings.

Over time, social collectives establish norms for which lines of action can be produced within certain routines, and they typically convert these norms into social laws and institutionalized practices (e.g., social roles) that get passed down historically in cultural forms of behavior. Everyone who enters a community-through birth or joining-necessarily enters into a historical sphere of tacit agreements about what can and cannot constitute "the real." One does not merely accept ideas about the world; one agrees to also act accordingly, to "do things as we do them".

Second, by terms of tradition, these social forms of behavior are passed along through historical lineages of interaction that are necessarily infused with meaning potentials. Social actors need some method by which to identify and perform particular lines of action, and social acts constitute the available forms of action with which social actors can work.

These forms of action will be encountered, interpreted, and learned through interactions with others who have been producing and working with them throughout their lives. They will pass along not just the mere form of behavior but the understandings that they have encountered and reproduced in their own enactments of these social acts. Some noted that all forms of social behavior thus bring into being modes of social participation: The child grows up within the order and customs of the family which it shares with other members and its mother's orders are accepted in this context.

Before it learns to talk it is already wholly immersed in that common medium. It learns to understand the gestures and facial expressions, movements and exclamations, words and sentences, only because it encounters them always in the same form and in the same relation to what they mean and express. Thus the individual orients himself in the world of objective mind.

Third, traditional and meaning-infused lines of available social action will be regulated and distributed through social roles. Here, social roles are seen as lines of action that must be configured with those of other social roles. The role, in a sense, is a device by which social actors can interpret and configure the overall line of action of the routine.

Because a role is only a partial and participatory line of action within a routine, it creates and enables only a partial degree of meaning-making and understanding that is necessarily dependent upon other role performances. Each social actor thus has a supervised and limited degree of autonomy in meaning production and, therefore, a severely constrained and dependent means of understanding available in any given social situation.

Finally, the grammatical nature of social routines establishes constraints on what lines of action can be produced and sensibly incorporated with other lines of action. Lines of social action are constrained by the need to be sensibly performed and incorporated into a given routine in order to maintain the codability of the routine.

Just as a sentence needs a certain grammatical format in order to be produced and recognized as a sentence, so does a routine need a certain grammatical format in order to be produced and recognized as a routine. One cannot, for example, sensibly make "Monopoly moves" in the context of a chess game.

In this respect, media-related forms of interaction also bring significant constraints to encounters with media content. The conditions by which content will be encountered, attended to, and interpreted are derived from historically perpetuated forms of available action that potentially enact a host of other social acts and interconnected meaning possibilities. The particular forms of media actions in which social actors can participate are made available by the particular social routine being produced and the coding and decoding necessities of that routine.

There is not, then, an "anything goes" philosophy of interpretation or media-related action that can permeate the media experience. Media-related interactions and understandings for media content must necessarily reenact cultural conventions and potentially reproduce socially supervised meanings. The mere act of, say, watching television brings with it a history of interactions and a host of local contingencies that continue to modify the experience. Social actors will necessarily be responsible to their immediate proceedings and their interactions with social others, and their decodings must sensibly fit with what takes place.

5. Historic social constraints and, hence, the terms for decoding media content, can nevertheless be modified through reflexive reconstructions of social routines

Clearly, the social practices that produce and reproduce social meanings reflect macroscopic dimensions, and these have significant and concrete effects on people's lives. Ultimately, however, these dimensions exist and are encountered only in concrete manifestations of social behavior that necessarily emerge as routines. Rules, laws, roles, etc. have their degrees of force only in enactments of social behaviors that get produced and reproduced in a variety of ways in relation to the contingencies at play in local settings. In this regard, these cultural forms of behavior do not wield influence as external forces per se. Here, for example, Blumer is adamant that legitimacy for cultural and structural variables be granted only with the inclusion of the concrete manifestations of behavior in which they appear:

> Conceptual schemes that depict society in some other fashion can only be derivations from the complex of

ongoing activity that constitutes group life. This is true of the two dominant conceptions of society in contemporary sociology-that of culture and that of social structure.

Culture as a conception, whether defined as custom, tradition, norm, value, rules, or such like, is clearly derived from what people do. Similarly, social structure in any of its aspects, as represented by such terms as social position, statuses, role, authority, and prestige, refers to relationships derived from how people act toward each other.

These social variables can rise and fall in different situations and their different configurations of action can start, stop, alter, etc. They are met in many forms and can call for new kinds of responses or alterations of old ones. Indeed, social actors can still manage a variety of meaning possibilities by performing the same lines of social behavior with different meanings. For example, a business meeting can be enacted in the guise of a ski trip. Such changes arise as social actors reflexively reinterpret and reconstruct the terms of their routines and the culturally provided forms of social behavior that characterize their performances. The different meanings produced for these social behaviors, in their turn, can redirect the overall atmosphere of meanings with which the social actors can work to interpret their world.

What culture intends, then, and what people do are not necessarily self-evident from people's words and actions. The meanings produced and used in media-related interactions will also be derived from how social actors bring their routines into being, and such reflexive improvisations can reconstruct the meanings produced in media-related interactions. It is not the mere forms of media-related behaviors that direct the media experience but also the methods of their enactment. "Watching TV" can be a sign of entertainment, ideological resistance, social competence, or avoidance of interpersonal conflicts.

Whatever meanings get produced for media-related behaviors necessarily redirect media decodings. One cannot assume, for example, that the mere reproduction of media discourse or behavioral displays automatically constitutes the reproduction of media-provided ideologies. It may be possible to, say, resist or reconstruct certain ideological or questionable presentations through their reproductions (e.g., reproducing media discourse in a satirical or sarcastic fashion as part of a routine that mocks the system).

These arguments about social behaviors and prescriptions provide grounded responses to Carragee's claims that (1) accommodation media approaches ignore significant matters of history, social power, etc. and (2) accommodation media approaches inappropriately emphasize social situations, sometimes at the expense of central meanings offered by content. First, it was shown that the theoretical bases of accommodation media ethnographies provide for studying matters of ideology and social-historical constraints. This provision assumes social actors will necessarily draw upon behavior conventions that preexisted the social actors. Such conventions are needed to make social action codable and decodable in recognizable terms. They will be encountered, practiced, and infused with meaning potential through forms of interaction.

In order to these constraints, accommodation scholars study social situations. It is only in studying these situations that any historic or political influences can be observed in concrete behavior. At the same time, the meanings of these social behaviors must not be presumed. Whereas they can constrain meaning, they are not necessarily determinative influences per se. Social actors may work with socially provided forms of behavior, but such behaviors must be brought into being through interpretation, configuration, and coordination. These behaviors, then, will have their meaning and force only in relation to their signifying characteristics in given constellations of action.

Social situations are not mere settings (or arenas) where social actors and media content magically appear and begin to simply act through motivations, etc. Social situations are the social regulatory devices that both enable and constrain the social "realities" and, hence, the ideological frameworks, that social actors use. In this regard, social actors cannot be conceptualized as ahistoric beings who act autonomously with individual subjectivities that direct either their own or collective courses of action.

They act, rather, within and through the necessities of coding and configurating localized actions. This need for meaning production and management also makes clear that any centrality of meaning in media content must be reconciled with any centrality of meaning in social situations. Looking only at the codified meanings of media content-or assuming these are always the only principal meanings with which audiences contend-ignores the other meanings social actors produce for themselves, their behaviors, and their surroundings in the course of situational action. The potential meanings of content have to be reconciled with the potential meanings of action. Audiences' management efforts could direct audience behaviors in ways that cannot be predicted from content alone.

The terms of encountering and decoding media content arise with and through forms of media-related interactions that do not structure the media experience per se but, rather, establish a set of meaning possibilities within which the social actors may have some range of negotiation. The central issue in such a view is not, then, how various social forces directly shape and limit the media experience. The issue, rather, is how the social actors collectively meet, enact, reenact, manage, and direct the terms of these potential forms of experience.

The socially constructed realities of audiences factor into an overall matrix of possible social experiences and opportunities. These are worthy of inclusion in any ethnographic media study. It is important, however, to differentiate research agendas from theoretical and methodological capabilities or directives. At this level, at least three significant research complications need to be addressed.

First, as Carragee's analysis contends, accommodation media studies have not engaged media content or audiences with the same levels of ideological concern that characterize cultural media studies. It does not necessarily follow, however, that the manner in which accommodation theories and ethnographies get conducted preclude examinations of particular social dimensions at fundamental levels. Hermeneutic investigations are-by their nature-directed by particular questions and objectives.

Here, it should be acknowledged that accommodation media approaches emerged within an atmosphere of American media studies that seemed preoccupied with structural and psychological theories and methods. These types of studies were deemed artificial or limiting in their approaches. In their quest to direct attention to the value and manner of studying social situations, accommodation media ethnographers might well have-in their terms-taken for granted what is so often implied in their premises.

If, in other words, the traditional, historic, and culturally constrained nature of social behavior was never addressed, it may be because this was simply assumed to be the nature of the beast. In this respect, some of the accommodation media ethnographies that were criticized in Carragee's analysis may need to be reexamined. Such work is currently being initiated.

Second, as indicated, the accommodation philosophy does not exclude the possibility that certain kinds of social situations can invite a select set of decodings for media content that could be viewed as "intended". A directive to study such meanings could make sense in these conditions, but such a directive must be tempered by a number of other considerations. How can such meanings come to be central or remain central in the course of any given routine?

Must the meanings produced for media content remain limited to a single range of possibilities? Is it feasible for social actors to maintain such a limited range under all social conditions, or are there only particular social conditions where these central meanings could be feasibly worked into social actions? Could these meanings be altered, amended, abandoned, returned to, or otherwise linked with other socially produced meanings in any given routine or across a range of routines?

Third, the study of socially provided conditions is also a legitimate directive. It is difficult to dispute that social resources are unevenly distributed and could potentially limit audience possibilities. If you cannot afford a newspaper or cable, for example, you work within a set of contingencies that provide for only certain kinds of media experiences. On the other hand, providing all of the best resources is no guarantee that those resources will be managed in the most efficient ways.

What needs to be studied is not so much social structures as the terms of tradition that might infuse media-related forms of interaction with particular meaning possibilities. Techniques are needed by which to conduct cross-generational analyses of these forms. If media-related behavior is part of a lineage of interactions and ways that audience collectives construct their media experiences, it would be useful to know how these lineages are being produced or reconstructed over time. Caution is clearly needed, however, to avoid presumptions of what audience activities mean. To see particular forms of meaning construction as "resistance," is a potentially useful hermeneutic device. The device must nevertheless be reconciled with other possible meanings for forms of audience behavior that audiences might produce.

"Resistance," for example, might also be a form of "play" or be transformed as such.

Conceptualizing and advancing such research will necessarily require a different spirit of comparison between accommodation and other forms of media study, especially cultural studies approaches. If the central issue in all of this research concerns audiences, it seems appropriate that the doors of communication and cooperation be opened as wide as possible to accommodate audiences' needs and interests.

An encouraging sign is that some cultural studies ethnographers are now considering the merits of what behavior sign systems might have to contribute. Certainly, a fruitful alliance between the approaches still requires that accommodation media ethnographies be examined in the strictest possible ways. It is hoped that such examinations will continue to be conducted with open- minded regard to their merits and potentials.

Representation of Ethnic Minorities

A great deal of the literature on the representation of ethnicity focuses one-sidedly on the representation of ethnic minorities. This is not only absurd, but in a sense almost runs the risk of helping to reproduce the problem. It is absurd because it implies that the ethnic minority group in question is somehow defined in a social vacuum, rather than in relation to another dominant term in the social equation-or even terms, because often there is more than one ethnic minority significantly placed in the social structure. And implicitly, such an approach may suggest that the 'minority' in question is indeed somehow a lesser moon circling the central, 'normal' planet of the nation in question, rather than an integral if not integrated force within that nation.

There are of course many historical studies of imperial self-definitions; some studies, albeit contested, of slave holder self-understanding; and studies of racial hegemony and the ideology of racial exceptionalism in Latin America. These are important for media definitions and flows, because even though they have little or no direct media or contemporary significance, they analyse the wellsprings upon which current discourse largely draws.

The public definition of the ethnic majority in that region is quite often based upon the notion of nationality rather than ethnic group, though not universally or strictly so in relation to all ethnic groups. Indeed, to some significant extent perhaps even the persistence of sectarian identifications represents a religious flask with nationalist content. In turn, national self-identification implies the right to an autonomous state structure, something claimed in Western Europe-Basques, Scots-only rather half-heartedly by Eastern European and CIS standards. This national self-identification also often involves a claim to traditional territory, the Potato Principle as Gellner has rather acerbically put it: 'allocation of a given territory should be determined by where a population lived in the agrarian era.'

Settled Ethnic Minorities

This term is used here to differentiate for the purposes of discussion, so far as it is valid to do so in a given instance, an ethnic minority group whose members are settled elements in the society rather than (a) recent migrant workers or refugees or (b) members of a marginalised indigenous group. For this analysis we are keeping the three defined categories distinct, even though in some instances there is, inevitably, overlap-for example in the persistence of the term 'immigrant' in British and French discourse to signify a person of colour. Classic examples of a settled ethnic minority group would be African Americans and Afro-Brazilians, whose presence in the Americas long predates the Asian, and Eastern and Southern European migrations to the USA and Brazil of the latter 19th century.

This area is the one where the most research has been done, and thus it is the hardest to summarise without diving into a morass of detail. Let us begin by listing the typical themes that have emerged from these studies, often organised along rather diverse conceptual axes. Amongst those which we will address below are:

1. *The historical/colonial cultural legacy*: and its role in shaping territorial boundaries and contemporary identities.
2. *The social class dimension*: and its significance in relation to the exercise of power within the state and globally; and its fracturing of ethnic and gender identities.
3. *The overlap between racial, sectarian, and linguistic factors and stereotypes*: there is a need for analytic clarity in refusing to reduce all discriminatory processes to racism.
4. *The question of invisibility and voicelessness*: the denial of an autonomous capacity to speak for oneself is a recurrent experience of ethnic minority communities.
5. *The simplification and homogenisation processes involved in media stereotyping*: media producers and their audience routinely operate with a partisan acceptance of stereotypes which legitimate the status quo.
6. *Problems of partial, intermediate, and inflected recognition in media output*: the development of 'multicultural' policies in modern states often generates new and subtle stereotypes which sustain the existing inequalities.
7. The interrelation between discourse and representation concerning foreign nations or even continents, and concerning 'fragments' of those entities settled inside the nation in question, require a continuous awareness of the interplay of the processes of construction of the alien 'other' located beyond the territory of the state,

> and the related processes of defining the majority dominant identity within the state. In this process the ethnic minority is typically constructed as the ambiguous stranger within 'our' midst.

The historical/colonial cultural legacy has already been addressed in relation to the representation of ethnic majorities.

The area of particular relevance to the theme in the Americas and Australia is, of course, the portrayal of indigenous land-based peoples and nations, which will be discussed below. Now, however, may be as appropriate a moment as any to address two standard problems in academic analysis, so far as we are concerned: (1) the issue of 'orientalism' and (2) the discourse of 'The Other.'

Edward Said's contributions to the analysis of racist and colonialist discourse have been masterful, and we are not seeking to dispute them here. The problem is more in the utilisation of his work, namely the subsumption of all such discourse under the single heading of 'orientalism.' The strength of Said's work lies precisely in its specificity about the region in question, the ineptly-titled 'Middle' East. Colonialist images and discourse about South or East Asia, about Africa or Latin America, sometimes may resonate with their counterparts elsewhere, but need not do so at all.

The terminology of 'The Other' is also in our view frequently problematic, though we would not go so far as to term it fatally flawed. Its strength primarily resides in its analysis of how social actors construct difference, which has a bearing on a very wide range of social interaction, not merely between different ethnic groups. However, it is perhaps in its over-use that we see a major difficulty: it implies that difference in and of itself generates negative responses, which would seem very strange to George Herbert Mead for example, for whom interaction with the Other is how we first come to be socialised into maturity.

We would want to point to the necessity of fully locating self and other in a historically developed social and cultural context, and to retain a sense of the complexity of 'the other.' Bauman has done much to develop a richer understanding of the psychological and social ambiguity of 'otherness.'

Furthermore, and in line with the sub-topic of the colonial cultural legacy, the point is precisely that the colonised are not alien, and are thought, however misguidedly, to be very well known. Perhaps particularly when settled in the midst of the majority society as settled ethnic minorities they constitute that awkward category of stranger, rather than the more easily contained, and invented, category of alien. They are known, but not of us, and may perhaps be able to make legitimate demands that could be more easily denied the alien. There is a whole stereotypical space in the culture for them to fill, just as there is in European and American cultures for Jews and Gypsies. Their personal physical presence is not needed for the stereotype to continue, and indeed is always a threat to the stereotype if normal social ties are developed across ethnic barriers.

Social class defined as a relational dynamic rather than as a static descriptor, is also an important dimension in media coverage, albeit rarely explicitly. Perhaps our point can best be summarised initially by three remarks.

(a) Crime, violence and other problems of social order are especially associated with media representation of ethnic minority groups.

(b) Historically, whether in the USA, Britain or other nations, certain types of legally defined crime have been much more prevalent in certain social classes than others. Street robbery, hooliganism, public disturbance, and similar types of offence have been common in working class neighbourhoods, while embezzlement, fraud and blackmail have been the genteel and infinitely more lucrative speciality of bourgeois classes.

Insofar as ethnic minority groups overlap with the working class, and inasmuch as they tend to be members of an extruded group within that class, subjected to high rates of discrimination, unemployment and low wages as, the Irish in 19th century Britain and the United States-then there is sociologically likely to be a greater incidence of working class forms of criminality among them. This incidence, however, has repeatedly been ascribed in public discourse to genetic and more recently also to cultural factors overwhelmingly associated with the given ethnic minority group. Intermittent 'moral panics' break out, sometimes perhaps orchestrated or at least oiled, sometimes not, concerning the threat to the social order constituted.

(c) August Bebel once defined anti-Semitism as 'the socialism of the idiot,' meaning that a primitive anger against exploitation targeted a partially visible minority, Jews, rather than socio- economic structures, as the cause of injustice. Once again, we have an example of a racist displacement of social class processes. While direct anti-Semitism is currently rare in the official media of Western Europe, the USA, Canada and Australia, it would be a mistake to assume no reversion is possible.

The question of linguistic and sectarian issues overlapping with 'racial' issues in the media is also an important one. The point is fairly obvious, but media and other public discourse concerning the use of Spanish in the United States, or concerning the role of Islam in Europe, are both significant issues that touch simultaneously on ethnic majority self-perceptions and on definitions of ethnic minority groups.

Invisibility and voicelessness have repeatedly been shown to be characteristics of media coverage-or non-coverage-of subordinate ethnic group issues. Either the whole ethnic group is invisible, or it is visible in certain highly specific manifestations, or it is spoken for and about by non-members, or individuals or organisations are selected by mainstream news professionals as regularly accredited spokespeople for the group in question. In this manner, communication media frustrate and defeat the possibility of representative dialogue within the public sphere.

Ethnic stereotypes, like all social cognition, simplify and homogenise complex realities. The problem with them is not this in itself, but (a) the simplification is in a negative cast, even when it may initially have the semblance of being positive and (b) whereas in many areas the dissection of complexity is also prized as a necessary complement to simplification, in the arena of race relations it is typically avoided as otiose. The precise stereotypes vary with the particular ethnic minority group, be they Mexican Americans or Algerians or Jews or Turks. This in part supplies them with their tenacity, in that they appear to have some genuine purchase upon very specific empirical realities. Their essence is not thought possible for its category members to escape, and exceptions are always taken to prove the rule. Indeed a part of the vitality of stereotypes in use is their capacity to operate as fragmented images capable of assembly and disassem bly into endless pragmatic conglomerates of meaning.

One of the most important but difficult issues to examine is what might be termed the second phase of ethnic group representation in media coverage: the point at which protests and critiques begin to lodge in media organisations' planning, and the representations change from the grossest deformations to more sophisticated ones. This is a classic area of 'half-empty versus half-full' analyses.

Lastly, on fragment cultures images and discourses of Africa, Latin America, Asia, and the 'Middle' East undoubtedly also have a major impact upon the public culture in metropolitan countries given the tendency to essentialism that is endemic in racist ideology.

News and Race Relations

Indeed, a key methodological issue for media flows research is also precisely how best to handle the inter-textual chorus—what to do about cinema, advertising, public relations, and entertainment media in relation to the news categories that have tended to be the predominant focus of such research. The image of the chorus should not be overstretched, as a number of these thematic and ideological interconnections are dissonant, not functionally harmonious.

One of the issues then that media flows research has to address is whether it suffers from an overly 'rational-cognitive' academic bias in its tendency to focus on news and journalistic representations. The underlying presumption seems sometimes to be that a 'facts vs non-facts' expose will bring the house of cards tumbling down, and while we would not wish to discount the merits of such exposes, or to downplay the rational in favour of mere assertion, exposes cannot be expected to be overwhelming in their effects.

Having said that, it is nonetheless the case that news media are of massive significance in the daily communication of what purport to be the realities of 'race.' Different topics may predominate in different national media, with 'immigration' being to the forefront in European news values over the past three decades, and questions of civil rights and crime occupying centre stage in the United States, while other nations' news media may vary again.

If there is a single finding that keeps on being replicated, it is that events and processes are described without being explained. Protest and riot are given dramatic pictures and gritty detail, but their causes are never made understandable. It might be said with justification that this is in part a product of the conventional processes of news gathering, and not a specific decision to reject explanations in the particular zone of public life. However, hand-in-hand with this superficiality goes a steady refusal to put the realities of discrimination and racism centre stage as news items. In this way, media assist in the perpetuation of racism by effectively keeping its harsh realities muffled in the public sphere. Indeed, much academic discourse concerning the public sphere equally obliterates the concerns of racially extruded groups from its analyses.

Ultimately, the task of media flows research in relation to ethnic issues is probably to isolate out the major constructs utilised in public discourse that refract and in so doing marginalise the legitimate concerns of ethnic minority groups-constructs such as immigration, crime, loyalty to the state, undue economic power-and to connect these to the working relationship between the power structure and mainstream media. For news analysis in particular, that power relationship may be said to be peculiarly significant, though to take different and often complicated forms depending upon whether reference is being made to the economic or the political power structure, and in which society.

Husband in synthesising the implications of the regional studies gathered under the Media and Refugees work identified a number of major factors relating to the informational needs of refugees. These included a necessary identification of target audiences and the use of media appropriate to their circumstances and experience. Informational needs were seen as falling into a number of categories reflecting the different priorities of particular stages of the arrival and settlement process. Clearly the informational needs on first arrival are highly specific and pragmatic and related to the immediate anxieties of survival and adaptation to the strange environment. Subsequent informational needs reflect the desire to acquire cultural and social competence in the receiving society in order to claim and exercise personal autonomy. And simultaneously there is a need to retain a communicative link with their 'home' country as both a necessary means of sustaining the viability of return and as an important mechanism of maintaining collective identity whilst in exile.

Asylum seekers and refugees are continuing distressing phenomenon in our contemporary world. Many of the poorer nations of the world carry a disproportionate share of the social and economic burden of providing asylum, whilst the wealthier nations employ the serendipitous consequences of geography and draconian policies robustly enforced to minimise their role as receiving countries. The role of the mass media in sustaining an ignorant fatalism in regard to the origin of refugee crises, and a popular veneer of humanitarian concern, massaged by voluntarism and state tokenism, should not be underestimated. Too often the abuse of human rights in creating refugee situations, and the collusive denial of the expression of responsibilities under human rights international instruments, are both perpetrated and legitimated through an ideological cocktail of nationalism, racism, and economic self-interest. The communicative rights of refugees cannot be detached from the broader context of human rights agendas which define the refugee's status and condition. As the UN High Commissioner for Refugees, Mrs. Sadako Ogata said in her address to the 1993 session of the Commission on Human Rights.

The issue of human rights and the problems of refugees are so inextricably linked that it is hardly possible to discuss one without referring to the other. Human rights violations are a major cause of refugee flows and also a major obstacle to the solution of refugee problems through voluntary repatriation. More positively, safe-guarding human rights is the best way to prevent conditions that force people to become refugees; respect for human rights is a key element in the protection of refugees in their country of asylum; and improved observance of human rights standards is often critical for the solution of refugees problems by enabling refugees to return safely home.

With the dramatic changes in the European economy in the 1970s and the rapid introduction of 'Immigration stop' policies throughout western European states, there have been two decades now of virtually no primary migration for employment into these states. However, contract labour and patterns of seasonal migration still exist as major features of the labour market in other continents. And within western Europe there are still those who find themselves in anomalous situations like the Turkish community in Germany. As Brubaker has indicated, the fundamental distinction in migrant situations is not that between citizen and non-citizen, but that between immigrant and non-immigrant. It is the immigrant status with 'permanent resident' qualification (USA), or 'indefinite leave to remain' (UK), or 'Carte de Resident' (France) which most fundamentally distinguishes the social and labour situation of non-citizen from non-citizen.

The non-citizen on contract, or the undocumented alien, lacks the substantive citizenship rights usually available to the recognised immigrant. It is the latter who have no need of special permission to work and if unemployed do not face expulsion. The economic, political, and social circumstances of the contract guest worker are routinely heavily qualified by the terms of their entry into the country and their terms of employment. Unlike naturalised ethnic minorities and communities of migrants with permanent resident status these workers are not conceived of as communities by the receiving country. Their formal transitory status renders them as not relevant to policies of assimilation or integration which may be deemed appropriate to stable multi-ethnic politics.

In multi-ethnic societies with stable ethnic minority communities it has frequently been the case that the state has developed information strategies aimed at facilitating the integration of the minority community into the receiving society. A Unesco supported comparative analysis of 'The Role of Information in the Realisation of the Human Rights of Migrant Workers' provides comparative examples of such policies. Typically such communication policies have employed a definition of multiculturalism which has privileged the cultural identity of 'the nation' and has promoted an informational flow which obviated addressing power relations and racism in the multi-ethnic society. Less frequently the receiving society, or more accurately the dominant ethnic community, has initiated policies aimed at facilitating the autonomous communicative activity of ethnic minorities. However, here too the dominant ethnic communities concern to protect their privileged status has heavily compromised such initiatives.

The status and temporal ambiguity of contract labourers has rendered them marginal to such policies, or has engendered communication policies premised upon a concern to facilitate their return to their 'homeland,' as in the case of the Federal Republic of Germany's policies toward 'Gastarbeiters.' For such migrants informal social networks are likely to be a critical element in their informational environment. Indeed for some contract workers their rights of assembly and freedom of communication may be heavily circumscribed and their capacity for social and cultural expression be severely limited. Thus it is important to note that the Unesco supported programme had as its starting point and guiding ethos a human rights basis for its concern with the communication environment of migrants. This starting point lay in the Final Act of the Conference on Security and Co-operation in Europe in which the special needs of migrant workers were acknowledged in confirming their right 'to receive, as far as possible, regular information in their own language, covering both their country of origin and the host country.'

Indigenous Groups

The use of the concept of indigenous groups immediately raises a number of issues. Notions of aboriginality, territoriality, and nationhood all immediately take on a temporal and historical relevance. The relation of people in terms of a collective ethnic identity, their relation to their native land, and the primacy of their claim to autonomous self-government all take on meaning only in relation to a parallel history of invasion, immigration, settlement, and the subsequent resting of political and economic power from the indigenous peoples by immigrants to their territory. Indeed the history of patterns of settlement itself leads to a hierarchy of claims to determining the ethnic authenticity of the nation. For example, the Anglo-fragment societies constructed through British colonial expansion have a strong sense of founding 'charter groups' who 'made' these countries.

The process of invasion/immigration, domination, and legitimation of the new order has typically resulted in a marginalization, and often planned or de facto cultural devastation, of the indigenous peoples. Subsequent patterns of immigration have been under the control of, and in the interest of, the Charter Groups, with the aboriginal peoples being further squeezed territorially and politically through this accommodation between the Charter Groups and newcomers.

Not surprisingly the multicultural policies of the 1970s and 80s have reflected the primacy of this relationship, with the labour needs of the national economy modifying the Charter Groups old ethnocentric sentiments and racist policies in order to sustain growth; and consequently there has been active intervention by the state in seeking to negotiate 'harmonious community relations. Within multicultural policies the indigenous peoples constitute an awkward category. Their historical oppression, both economically and culturally, typically leaves them with a demography unlike that of the original usurpers or the more recent immigrant populations. Like the Samis in Norway, the Aboriginals in Australia, and the Native Peoples of North America they are often geographically and socially isolated and have a disadvantaged relation to both the labour market and political institutions. Not surprisingly indigenous peoples have chosen to detach themselves from the collusive invention of national identity implicit in the invaders multiculturalism.

The representation of indigenous peoples in the majority media is an expression of their incorporation into the foundation myths of the contemporary state. There is, for example, the 'pre-modern' noble-savage whose simple certainties and arcane knowledge compare favourable with the sophistication, rationality, and complexity of our current era.

Of course the other major form of representation of indigenous groups is through their invisibility in mainstream media, outside of their visibility as 'problems' or 'victims' in the news media. Langton writing of Australia in 1992 notes that 'Aboriginal and Islander people were still virtually invisible on three commercial television networks'. It is the interactive impact of indigenous peoples absence from routine broadcast media and the particular and narrow, range of iconography attached to them in the news, and occasionally in film, that shapes their perception amongst majority communities and contributes to the alienation of indigenous people from the wider society.

When we consider the participation of indigenous peoples in media production a number of issues become salient. Almost ironically one of the issues is essentialist claims within the indigenous groups over who is able to 'authentically' generate representations of their collective experience and contemporary politics. There is a naive belief that Aboriginal people will make 'better' representations of us, simply because being Aboriginal gives 'greater' understanding. This belief is based on an ancient and universal feature of racism: the assumption of the undifferentiated other. More specifically, the assumption is that all Aborigines are alike and equally understand each other, without regard to cultural variation, history, gender, sexual preference and so on. It is a demand for censorship: there is a 'right' way to be Aboriginal, and any Aboriginal film or video producer will necessarily make a 'true' representation of 'Aboriginality.'

This thinking is as much based on fear of difference as is white Australian racism. Given the centuries of oppression and resistance to culture, and physical obliteration it is hardly surprising that in-group social identity should have become invested with all the accumulated anxiety and sensitivity associated with resistance and survival. Nor is it surprising that it may have incorporated something of the category-defining variables of the dominant oppressor. And, in the contemporary 'pork-barrel' funding of ethnic politics, it is also probable that essentialist claims have pecuniary and political advantage. In a context of endemic under-funding competition for the ethnic-dollar can be expected to be acute.

That some funding does exist is critical to both majority multiculturalism and indigenous peoples' media strategies. Such funding may be directly for indigenous peoples media activity, or indirectly attached through clauses in franchising commercial media. The former reflects the demography of relatively small, often isolated, communities and the latter indicates an intention to 'mainstream' provision. Both options are inherently defensible. Experience indicates some of the difficulties that may be encountered. Efforts to generate autonomous indigenous community media have faced a number of problems. A recurrent issue is their geographical dispersal and the linguistic diversity and the variation in life styles within indigenous populations. The diversity reflects itself not only in different agendas and aesthetics being brought to media production but it also significantly fragments potential audiences and may have serious implications for the financial viability of particular media initiatives. The two processes of production and consumption are of course not independent.

A significant feature of that production in traditional groups has to do with the involvement of those people who have the authority to produce the image or tell the story. Aboriginal Law governs wider production in much the same way as in any other area of life.

That Aboriginal groups in 'settled' Australia have not been able to achieve the same degree of control over content and dissemination is a reflection of their different legal status outside of areas governed by Traditional Law and accessing media with different patterns of control and ownership. The BRACS matched technology to need.

That the nature of the funding base is equally critical was indicated by the struggle for Aboriginal control over the Remote Commercial Television Station at Alice Springs. Having won a prolonged struggle for control of the franchise, Imparja found that its commercial prerogatives had fundamentally undermined its aspirations of serving Aboriginal audiences. Batty estimated that in the whole of 1991 only 6.5 hours of programming in Aboriginal languages was transmitted.

Funding of technology is not the same as funding production, and the interests represented in extending the reach of telecommunications and broadcast systems are not coterminous with the interests of the intended beneficiary audiences. Capital grants for start up technology have a different logic and financial trajectory to commitments to sustain indigenous production; as the situation in remote Australia and Northern Canada in different ways have indicated. And in all instances the indigenous peoples have shown a desire, and often an ability, to exercise control of local programming. Indigenous peoples communication environment is closely related to their economic, demographic and political characteristics. The total neglect, or wanton abuse, of indigenous peoples does not have the explicit consensual support of earlier colonising ideologies of racial superiority or confident assertions of terra nulius.

The latter part of the twentieth century has seen an international recognition of the distinctive identities of indigenous peoples and explicit concern with their human rights: as for example in the 1993 Vienna Declaration following The World Conference of Human Rights. In a number of 'settler' societies these international sentiments and the political mobilisation of their indigenous peoples have become focused into an awkward renegotiation of the relationship between the charter groups and the indigenous peoples. This is often associated with a broader renegotiation of national identity: Australia and the Mabo case being a particular instance. Thus indigenous peoples can currently be seen to seek to exploit contemporary communications technologies to defend their identity and community whilst simultaneously trying to achieve controlled access to the wider society. Regardless of the technology or the locality it is control of production and distribution which is recurrently central among their concerns.

Mainstreaming Media

There ought to be no such concept as 'mainstream media' in functionally egalitarian multi-ethnic societies: that is not to say there would be no ethnically distinctive media. However, the national print or broadcast media would, like the society itself, be multi-ethnic in staffing, programming values and content. They would not, as now, be essentially coterminous with the aesthetics and interests of the dominant ethnic groups, charter or otherwise. At present the conception of mainstream media inevitably juxtaposes a hegemonic orthodoxy against a problematic heterogeneous range of ethnic identities and politics. To speak of a society enjoying the complementary benefits of multi-ethnic and dedicated ethnic media is not compatible with speaking of 'mainstream' and 'ethnic minority' media.

However, in the context of the current mainstream media the ubiquitous penetration of the values and interests of the dominant ethnic communities is apparent. Speaking of the Australian situation Seneviratne has identified the significance of accent as a sufficient hindrance to participation in the mainstream. Many highly skilled and experienced radio broadcasters of ethnic backgrounds have found the ABC's concept of 'style and standard' has been a formidable barrier as far as their access to the ABC's airways is concerned, because unless you have an 'Australian' accent, you are judged to be 'unprofessional.'

ABC applies a peculiar brand of programme standards where an 'ethnic' accent is okay if you are the person being interviewed, but the same accent is deemed to be not of broadcasting standard, if you want to be the interviewer, the presenter or the narrator of the programme. This certainly has a close similarity to British television which has a significant number of 'ethnic minority' news readers and journalists who seemly are expected to compensate for their deviant ethnicity by having ultra-orthodox BBC, or received pronunciation, accents.

A further significant aspect of the mainstream broadcasters pragmatic employment of minority personnel is identified by Downing and Ngui. They note the existence of a situation in which highly visible ethnic minority broadcasters find themselves in effect fronting for institutions within which ethnic minority persons are singularly absent from executive positions. This particular form of strategic tokenism places those ethnic minority professionals in an invidious position both personally and professionally. Personally they may feel isolated in a working environment in which they remain permanently 'exotic,' and professionally they may feel compromised through having to persistently work against the grain of the hegemonic political and cultural values which are normative within the system. And indeed, as Downing indicates, this ethnic veneering of broadcasting institutions has further implications for prospective ethnic minority employees, for his analysis of the American situation reveals networking to be a critical element in media career building.

One option which ethnic minority media workers have exercised has been to operate outside of the mainstream media, but to service its needs on a contract basis. This provides for a large degree of organisational autonomy and a strong sense of ethnic solidarity within the working environment. Clearly the mainstream is vulnerable to this strategy since whilst it needs to control its ethnic minority input it also has a need of the linguistic and cultural skills of ethnic minority professionals; and of their capacity to gain access to situations of conflict and stress from which mainstream professionals may well be excluded by physical threat or their cultural incompetence. Retaining a strong ethnic identity and credibility within the ethnic community and the careerist temptations of growing 'professional' success in servicing the mainstream are not easily reconciled. Maintaining an activist commitment whilst simultaneously negotiating professional and commercial success is a delicate process.

As in every other area of the interface of ethnicity with the operation and impact of media systems the mainstream media present a focus for the competing interests of a dominant ethnic hegemony and diverse ethnic minority interests. Ethnic minority communities are increasingly effectively penetrating the mainstream, whilst simultaneously threatening it by developing vibrant and viable ethnic minority media. This is a struggle in which the often ambiguous and neurotic identity of the dominant elite is vulnerable to internal doubt, and to the competing and autonomously disruptive impact of their own commercial imperatives perpetually in pursuit of an evolving fragmented audience. Pragmatic flexibiiity within the mainstream and coherent ethnic mobilisation by ethnic minorities would seem at present to offer a prospect of evolutionary change for the better.

Whilst specific variables may fruitfully be identified, and for pragmatic purposes be given independent analysis, the reality remains that it is only through an understanding of their contingent interaction that an adequate understanding may be achieved. Whilst there is a great deal of material examining the representation of ethnic minorities within the media its visibility and impressive quantity does not allow for such research to be regarded as redundant. The monitoring of the ever shifting metamorphoses of stereotypes and their incorporation in new and distinctive political discourse remains an important and continuing task. A comparative analysis of this process in relation to material, like the Cosby Show, transmitted into widely differing national and ethnic contexts is to be recommended.

The literature on cultural imperialism has appropriately focused attention upon international media flows, and yet the research reviewed above indicates the importance of monitoring intra-national flows across ethnic boundaries. And as the case of indigenous peoples amply demonstrates the intra-ethnic heterogeneity of world view, aesthetics and production capacity must also be reflected in analysis and research. The role of ethnic minority persons as agents of production and dissemination in the mass media requires urgent attention as a corrective to their being cast in the role of passive audiences and as a corrective to naive assumptions regarding uni-directional media flows.

Even a cursory glance at the pop music industry is sufficient to sense the complex interplay of creative market forces across national and ethnic boundaries. The cinema and literature offer further comparable instances, and the television industry in its deregulated and increasingly globalised form demands systematic comparative research. In all of these areas management and employment practices within media industries are essential aspects of media performance which are critical in an examination of racism and xenophobia within media industries. Here racism may be tapped in its most subtle and gross modes of expression.

This is particularly so since the arguments are often conflictual in their origin and expression there is no easy consensual framework for analysis which may be unthinkingly coopted. The interplay of racism, ethnicity, and the media requires an interdisciplinary analysis which permanently sees the part in relation to the whole.

Race, Nation and News

Defining the 'nation' long has been a contentious issue in the United States. Relatively clear and stable geopolitically, the idea of 'nation' becomes ambiguous and muddled on the sociocultural terrain. Belonging to a nation is both a legal and cultural issue. One can become a citizen of a nation, yet never be accepted within it culturally-or socially or politically.

In the United States, in the early 1900s, immigration from Asia led to intense nativism and, eventually, legislation that barred Chinese, Japanese, East Indians, and other Asian populations from moving to the United States. Members of those groups already in the United States were denied citizenship; some individuals were even denaturalized. The rationale for excluding East Indians from becoming part of the nation was typical of the reasoning offered by authorities: citizenship should be granted only to those people whose ancestors had lived in Europe and who would be "predisposed toward the United States' form of government".

During the 1980s, more than 9 million people entered the United States. A majority of documented immigrants between 1981 and 1990 came from Asia and Latin America. The impact of this immigration on American society was described in a recent Time magazine cover story. "Someday soon," the magazine declared, "...white Americans will become a minority group".

The demographic shifts that have resulted from the recent wave of immigration from Asia and Latin America have engendered conflict among racial groups for political power, jobs, and other increasingly scarce social and economic resources that historically have been controlled primarily by whites. Among the most tense of these conflicts are those between blacks and Latinos and between blacks and Asians. Blacks have asserted that Latino successes have come at their expense, while Latinos counter that blacks will not share with other minorities the benefits of civil rights victories. Tensions between blacks and Asian Americans in New York, Chicago, and Los Angeles also have increased.

The emerging demographic diversity in the United States has raised anew a number of fundamental questions about national identity and culture: What will the "new" multiracial and multicultural America look like? How will it be defined? What will it mean to be an American?

The meanings of the important sociological terms race and nation are social and political constructions and closely linked. The rhetorical arguments surrounding issues of national unity, national development, national citizenship, and national preservation, among others, frequently contain racially based arguments. Establishing and maintaining an imagined national community requires not only staking out geopolitical and cultural boundaries that become the basis for forming collective identity, but also popular agreement about who can and who cannot be considered legitimate members of the nation's citizenry. Ideas about inclusion and exclusion from the nation are often based on conceptions of racial superiority and inferiority. And these conceptions are, themselves, constructed ideas derived from perceived sociopolitical, economic, cultural and other needs and passions of a nation at a given historical moment.

Discourses about race and nation help create a national identity and racial hierarchy that often renders whiteness a sign of superiority and inclusion while relegating "people of color" to an inferior status, at times excluding them altogether from the social, political and cultural life of a nation. This racism can take two forms: Internal racism is directed against populations regarded as "a minority" within the nation and seeks to hierarchize and partition society.

External racism may take the form of xenophobia and may be associated with attempts to exterminate or eliminate those deemed inferior or with efforts to prevent them from immigrating. Because these forms of racial thinking are social constructions, they do not necessarily represent ideal types of behavior or structural forms so much as they do historical tendencies.

Nevertheless specific articulations between conceptions of race and the idea of nation can be identified. For example, in Anglo-European countries such as Great Britain, Australia, and the United States, the articulation is quite specific: those designated as non-whites become distinct "Others" whose perceived inferiority serves as the basis and justification for exclusion or oppression.

The news media, as a major source of cultural production and information, play a key role in the process of constructing meaning for race and nation. Journalists select certain issues, events, actors and sources for coverage and emphasis over others, and transform their selections into finished news items by identifying and contextualizing them in recognizable frames of reference.

As a result, news stories are imbued with meanings that help establish and maintain geopolitical and cultural boundaries of the nation and the racial criteria by which people are included in and excluded from it. While the content of news stories tends to support dominant definitions of key terms of social organization, the news media should not be viewed as a "relatively seamlessly reproducing apparatus consistently serving the entrenched powers".

There is some ideological flexibility in the extent to which the dominant definitions are supported in certain types of writing formats and publications. Columns and feature stories can more easily raise questions about dominant social definitions than can straight news stories. Publications with clear political commitments can present alternative perspectives more easily than can publications that profess to be objective and neutral purveyors of the news. Thus, the legitimacy of physical and cultural boundaries, the rigidity of hierarchies and social partitions, and vitriolic exclusionary rhetoric effectively can be undermined and challenged.

The journalism of race and nation might most productively be carried out, we should have a broad sense of the state of media and racial and ethnic minorities generally. First, in the United States, questions about racial and ethnic minorities generally are not considered important outside the context of their relations with whites. In most social science practice, the lives, culture and values of the racial and ethnic minorities gain significance only in their relationships with whites.

In mass communication study, for example, there have been a number of studies on how the press covered the Rodney King beating and the subsequent fallout. But these studies are almost always underpinned by a framework of Black-White relations, although the role of Koreans, Korean-Americans, and Latinos is usually acknowledged peripherally.

On racial and ethnic minorities often tends to be considered problematic by the academic community. The study is acceptable and more or less accepted as valid only to the extent that the findings conform to dominant conceptions of social organization and the place of the racial and ethnic minorities within that organization.

In sum, the primary reason for a lack of studies in the United States that critically assess news coverage of race and ethnicity is that many media researchers keep race and ethnicity at arm's length and generally avoid substantive questions about distributions of economic and political power; access to resources; and equality of opportunity organized along racial and ethnic difference. This problem is symptomatic of American society in general: most people do not want to talk openly and frankly about race and ethnicity because there is a popular perception in the United States that racist thinking is a thing of the past, eliminated by civil rights legislation and increasing tolerance for diversity.

If news treatment of racial and ethnic minorities is to be more meaningful, it must begin systematically to expose the enduring contradiction of life in the United States: the symbolic and material segregation and degradation of the racial and ethnic minorities in a liberal democracy that supposedly values equality and difference. To do that, media researchers need not only talk seriously and openly about race and ethnicity, but talk about race and ethnicity in ways that go beyond descriptive categories.

An initial step media researchers can take is to document by qualitative means the ways mass media segregate and degrade racial and ethnic minorities in the process of creating a sense of nation. This documentation cannot be done by counting heads and categorizing roles. Cultural geography, which takes on as one of its interests the study of the dispersion, interaction, and control of mobile populations suggests the types of questions that could guide qualitative work on news coverage of the race and nation: How do news media assign the racial and ethnic groups to certain spaces, places, and times? How do news media form hierarchies among and within groups? What are the implications of these spatial and temporal placements of the racial and ethnic minorities in terms of social control, public debate, and the meaning of citizenship and nation.

An alternative approach to the study of mainstream news media coverage of race and nation should take as a starting point that there is a particular racial ideology in the United States that structures journalistic practice and results in content that further perpetuates racial ideology. The racial ideology manifests itself in many ways in news coverage of racial and ethnic minorities. Two such manifestations to illustrate how racial ideology operates in news. These manifestations represent two strategies by which journalists writing for mainstream news media portray the intersection of race and nation: the depiction of racial hierarchy and the process of temporal distancing.

Racial Hierarchy

One of the enduring elements of U.S. racial ideology is the belief in a hierarchy of races with whites at the top and other races arrayed somewhere below. Racial hierarchy is characterized by specific features that tend to marginalize non-whites. For example, racial hierarchy tends to homogenize non-white racial groups into stereotypical overgeneralizations of their characteristics.

Racial hierarchy also implies that the cultural features

and sensibilities of racial groups higher in the hierarchy are superior and more valuable than those placed lower. Finally, racial hierarchy can "naturalize" superior or inferior positions because the hierarchy is supposedly constructed through "objective" methods, implying that the observed differences among racial groups are somehow "real".

One way news depicts racial and ethnic minorities as different from whites is through imagery that creates distance and isolation between the groups. These images of urban isolation and containment create distance between minority group, who are uniformly depicted as engaged in violence, crime, and conflict, and the predominantly white readers of the mainstream press, who, it is implied are living in safety and with civility in the suburbs.

However, racial minorities do not always represent a homogeneous bloc that is inferior to whites. There are distinct differentiations among the minorities based on perceived similarities between a specific racial group and whites. The U.S. mainstream news magazine coverage of interaction among racial and ethnic groups, found that whites, depicted as representing superior values, morals, and temperament, are consistently at the top, while blacks, an archetypical example of failed assimilation, are consistently at the bottom. Asian Americans and Latinos, however, hover somewhere in between whites and blacks, their specific placement determined by the extent to which they were perceived by the mainstream news magazines to be abiding by the established standards of thought and behavior appropriate for inclusion within the nation.

The process of differentiation is not limited to those drawn among racial or ethnic groups; there is some differentiation depicted within a racial or ethnic group. A study that examines how East Indians were depicted by the press during their fight for U.S. citizenship rights in the early 1900s, found a differentiation along lines of caste.

News coverage shows that all East Indians were despised by most white Americans, who supported judicial and legislative efforts to limit or eliminate East Indian immigration. However, there is almost a grudging respect in the news coverage for East Indians of upper caste backgrounds who are generally, academicians, philosophers, students, clergy, etc., as opposed to the East Indians from lower castes who immigrated to the United States as manual laborers.

Despite the differences in the depiction of elite and working-class East Indians painted by the news media, all were considered unfit for naturalization. "The Hindu is not a good citizen" declared the Bellingham Herald. Therefore, the news media reasoned, the "tide of turbans" must be excluded from the nation: "The process of dumping human derelicts on these shores will not be tolerated" wrote the editor of the San Francisco Call in 1910. East Indians already in the United States were depicted as the "hordes from India".

The portrayal of East Indians as belonging to a community characterized by political and class differences suggests that the process of inferiorizing is more complex than depicting a group as homogeneously inferior by simply listing a series of its undesirable characteristics. The mainstream news media depiction of interaction among minority groups suggested that different levels of "inferiority" are assigned to each racial minority. East Indians suggests that news representations of even a single racial minority group may differ along class divisions and political orientations, creating ever finer distinctions in racial hierarchy.

Temporal Distancing

Temporal distancing by the news media comprises two steps. First, the generic Other is symbolically isolated and placed at a distance from whites. Some found that Chicago area television news that "local news implicitly traces the symbolic boundaries of the community blacks are largely cast outside those boundaries." Black-Latino interaction, separation was accomplished by references to the "black ghetto" and to "Hispanic districts".

Similar usage of spatial imagery was found in a study of black-Asian American interaction. For example, one magazine used the following title in a article about Asian entrepreneurs in traditionally black neighborhoods: "Asian Merchants Find Ghetto Full of Peril: Koreans and Chinese Particular Targets in Inner city. During the rioting in the aftermath of the Rodney King verdict, Time magazine claimed that black-Korean American tension was inevitable because Koreans had "invaded the hear and soul of black America ". East Indians, they were depicted as living separate, self-segregated lives away from the rest of the community in what was labeled "Hindu towns".

The second step in temporal distancing is introducing a discourse of racial minorities as primitive, unsophisticated, backward, etc.-from a different time, not the modern present. Again, in the study of black-Latino interaction, blacks and Latinos are characterized as having "been left behind" by whites, in "another world" full of violence and conflict.

One way East Indians-especially the manual laborers were portrayed as inferior in news coverage was through the use of temporal symbols and images. News stories of diseased and dirty East Indians living in filthy shacks, of turbaned beggars belonging to a mystical race suggested that East Indians are primitive and belong in a different place and time, not in civilized, rational and modern early-20th century America. This racial "inferiorizing" of East Indians further strengthens the sense that the nation is for white Americans only and the brown East Indian, defined as being culturally, physically and mentally inferior, from a different place and time, and unwilling to assimilate, could never be a part of it, could never be a citizen.

This temporal imagery invoking the past creates cultural distance between the conduct of black-Latino interaction and the white majority while the imagery of space and isolation create symbolic physical distance. Thus, the two types of distance are related because the symbolic physical distance between Black-Latino interaction and the reader can be understood as reflecting sequence in time. As the symbolic physical distance between the reader and racial minorities grows, they recede into the reader's temporal past-a culturally distant past. Thus, the process of "temporal distancing" has the effect of making the "here and now" of the racial and ethnic groups the "there and then" of the reader.

U.S. mainstream news media coverage of racial minorities helps to stake out a cultural boundary that defines what it means to be American. And it means, at its core, being white and being superior over non-whites. The idea of Americans as superior is not accomplished by explicit enumeration of superior qualities. Rather, it is accomplished through the language of hierarchy and through spatial and temporal tropes. East Indians were portrayed as undesirable immigrants who should be excluded by legislation from the geopolitical unit called the United States. Blacks, Latinos, East Indians, and other Asians were represented as choosing to live apart and unwilling to assimilate, not wanting to belong to the nation. This depiction of domestic exclusion, an example of internal racism, was characterized, in part, by a racial hierarchy buttressed by a culturally and spatially distant privilege held by whites over non-whites.

The news depiction of racial hierarchy and the process of temporal distancing are among the ways journalism participates in the construction of race and nation. One of the results is meanings for race and nation that are highly institutionalized and profoundly ideological. They are institutionalized in the sense that they attain, through widespread dissemination and constant repetition, legitimacy and credibility as almost unquestionable cultural truths and are accepted as assumptions for formulating official and unofficial policies of exclusion. They are ideological because they serve to racialize the idea of immigration and citizenship. In other words, the ideas attain a racial meaning and become substitutes for talking directly and specifically about race.

Thus, racism per se can be denied, which makes it easier to argue that East Indians, Latinos, Asians, and other immigrants are being excluded from the nation not because of racism, but because the immigrants just cannot or will not assimilate. The ability to deny the existence of racism, then, is crucial for sustaining the idea of a nation built on the normative foundation of equality and fairness.

The denial of racism also makes it easier to ignore the contexts in which the desire to exclude minorities arises. The lack of context, the creation of classification schemes for excluding immigrants from certain parts of the world, and creating racial hierarchy among already-present minorities all tend to make social constructions such as race and nation appear somehow permanent, persistent, and natural.

10

Globalisation and Broadcast Media

Globalisation is a complex term that is understood differently by different people. For some scholars globalisation is understood as being mainly an economic process, e.g. as being the way in which the economies of various countries are becoming increasingly linked. For other scholars however, globalisation is a broader term that goes beyond the integration of economies, and for them globalisation can be described in terms such as "the confluence of economic, political, social, and cultural factors interacting on a world scale thanks to the expansion of knowledge, information, trade, and technology beyond geographic borders and poles of economic activity". Here the emphasis is on trans-border interactions involving different types of global forces.

A variation of this more encompassing perspective describes globalisation in terms of the different sectors within countries that these globalisation forces can impact on, e.g. specific industries, social and cultural systems, policies, or social reform processes aimed at achieving human development and human security. Globalisation is involving not only economic forces contributing to the integration of economies throughout the world, but also as involving other global forces that interact more broadly than just in the economic arena. This is in agreement with the approaches of most television policy makers world-wide.

Scholars who take the broader view of globalisation often differ with regard to which types of processes play the most important globalising role.

Someone who describes globalisation as a process whereby the world's people are becoming increasingly interconnected in all facets of their lives, states that economic processes such as international trade and investment are the main drivers of globalisation. On the other hand globalisation is greater in the cultural arena than in the economic or political arenas. These different approaches naturally have implications for how the impacts of global forces are perceived and for decisions on how local responses to globalisation are made. The importance of a specific global force would depend on what role-players and what sectors of society are taking into consideration. Just as beauty is said to be in the eye of the beholder, so can it be said that importance is in the minds of those making the judgement.

Decision makers who think that their interests are being affected substantially by a particular force to rate the importance of that force higher than would those who are less affected by it. Therefore, within any single industry the mind-sets of local decision makers play a major role in determining which global forces are seen as having an important enough impact in that industry to warrant some kind of response.

Globalisation A Social Process

Globalisation can be defined as a social process in which the constraints of geography on social and cultural arrangements recede, but at the same time it is a process in which people become aware that these constraints are receding. In other words globalisation processes operates on two levels. For Robertson, globalisation also takes place on two levels: firstly as compression of the world on a concrete level, and secondly as compression of the world on a socio-cultural level, where general views of life in terms of cognitions and values and "the intensification of consciousness of the world as a whole".

These views mean that any globalisation forces such as global economic changes or major technological developments can impact on local industries in two ways - directly and indirectly. An example of a global economic force that could have a direct impact on a local industry would be a drastic change in the international exchange rate of the local currency with regard to other currencies.

Indirect impacts of global forces are those impacts that are mediated by one or more intervening local variable, e.g. along the lines of weak economic determinism or weak technological determinism. These mediating socio-cultural variables are intangibles such as people's cognitions and values, e.g. the perceptions and attitudes of decision makers or other role-players in an industry affected by globalisation. For example, say there was a dramatic technological breakthrough that could enable countries world-wide to receive twice as many television broadcasts via satellite than previously.

In any particular country the impact of breakthrough would depend on if and how it was implemented locally, and in turn this would depend largely on local broadcasting decision makers' views of potential problems and benefits associated with the new technology. It therefore follows that socio-cultural variables such as the mind-sets of role-players in a particular industry not only help determine the perceived importance of global forces operative in that industry, but they also contribute largely to the local impact of and response to globalisation processes.

Different Types of Reactions to Globalisation

There are four types of people on the basis of how they tend to react to economic globalisation. Globalists are people who are in favour of economic globalisation but who believe that the global economy is now functioning in such a radically different way than before that the ability of nation states to combat this is significantly constrained.

Globalists' reactions to economic globalisation would typically include the restructuring of the local economy, the education and training of citizens so that they can compete effectively in the world economy, and policy changes that would enhance flexibility in labour markets. According to Ouattra of the International Monetary fund (IMF), those countries that have profited the most from economic globalisation are those that have responded with Globalist policy changes aimed at achieving macro-economic stability, promoting openness to trade and capital flows, and limiting government intervention to areas of genuine market failure.

The reaction to globalisation of those who could be classified as belonging to the Traditional Left, who are not in favour of economic globalisation, would be to resist further integration into the global order on unrestricted terms. They would, for example, insist on world trade being conducted in terms compatible with the preservation of local social and democratic values, e.g. by the insertion of social requirements into international trading agreements.

On the other hand, the reaction of the Keynesians, people who also are against economic globalisation, would typically be to reinforce existing structures and processes, e.g. by demanding more expansive macro-economic policies to increase the aggregate demand in external economies and to reduce the slack in labour markets.

Impacts of Globalisation

Among the risks often associated with economic globalisation is the fact that structural weakness in economies are exposed as investment capital seeks out the most efficient markets, while capital mobility could lead to destabilizing flows and heightened exchange rate volatility. Even for developed countries additional imports from lower-wage countries can shift production to other countries, hurting local wages and decreasing local job opportunities. Also, economic integration can occur at the cost of a reduced autonomy of the nation state: there could be a loss of economic and political sovereignty, and national economies and governments are vulnerable at the hands of international markets and international political economy.

A useful concept in the literature that sheds light on the dynamics of local reactions to global forces, is localisation. Localisation can be defined as a process that expresses the "need to maintain local or national control over the processes and pace of change". Localisation actions can therefore be seen as local reactions to external globalising forces, and depending on the geographical scope of the response, localisation actions can operate on different levels. Localisation actions are often a response to the fragmentation that could occur as a result of global forces' weakening effect on national or other borders. Integration on one level can often have a fragmenting effect on another level, e.g. the collapse of socialist nation states such as the USSR and Yugoslavia and their integration into the free world was accompanied by separatist tendencies and the emergence of smaller states.

Fragmentation can therefore be described as being the opposite of globalisation, but as it so often accompanies globalisation it also seems to be part of globalisation, and this reflects a paradox inherent to the process of globalisation. Localisation and globalisation can also be understood as the thesis and antithesis of a dialectic process that leads to change: The two interact directly and each functions as a causal source for the other.

Braman distinguishes between three types or phases of localisation processes : Primary localisation emanates mainly from a traditional environment in which the local is identified with physical place, and in which the local in its material forms constitutes culture. In such an environment, place is usually understood as the conjuncture of geographic, material and social forces as they come together to create a home. Secondary localisation is associated with a modernistic environment in which the local is defined as a culturally based reference point. It is secondary locality that drives tourism economically.

Tertiary localisation is emerging out of the postmodern condition in which the local is seen as a willed construct that is conceptually defined. It also involves the local as being increasingly grounded in experiences with virtual communities in cyberspace. It follows from this exposition that the type of localisation actions that societies make in response to globalisation will largely be determined by whether these actions emanate from a traditional, modern or postmodern environment.

Also instrumental in determining the scope and nature of localisation actions, are those aspects or dimensions of the local that are emphasised most in these actions. Braman mentions four such dimensions of the local: (a) geographic definition (physical properties that define local), (b) cultural and historical aspects of a geographic site (referred to as locale), (c) sites of human agency (locus), and (d) material features of a place that are reproducible elsewhere (location, as in a movie location). Should, the geographic dimension of a localisation response to globalisation be emphasised in such a way that is undertaken on a regional level across national borders, then that localisation action itself could be experienced in the adjacent areas as a new, and possibly negative, globalisation force inviting further reaction.

Some localisation actions on a regional level can therefore involve responding to globalisation in kind - like fighting fire with fire, but to the possible detriment of others in the adjacent areas of the region. Other types of regional responses could benefit all in the region. The potentially negative globalising effect on neighbouring countries of some regional localisation responses make such actions qualitatively different to national/smaller localisation actions. This means that our analysis of how television industries react to globalisation should clearly distinguish – in agreement with Straubhaar's distinction between different levels of television flows and impacts- between reactions on a global level, on a regional (larger than national) level, and those on a national or smaller scale. Within the broadcasting industry localisation measures on a regional level have, where possible to implement, usually proved to be an effective mode of response that benefited the country initiating the response.

Many developing countries have however chosen to rather go on the defensive against external global forces and have instituted regulations that are aimed at nurturing the growth of local industries or ensuring a level of economic autonomy. Depending on whether or not they are subject to a free trade treaty developed under the General Agreement on Trade and Tariffs (GATT) or the World Trade Organisation (WTO), such actions could be deemed illegal and then could not be exercised. Broadcasting is however, not subject to such GATT or WTO agreements. Sinclair et al. note that ever since the late 1970s, the global audio-visual landscape has increasingly been subject to four types of global forces of change:

— *Economic forces:* These included firstly some broad economic changes such as the rise of Asian economies and the move toward a post-Fordist mode of organisation of the economy in the Western world. This meant a push for more global trade liberation and competition on a national and international level, but less centrality of the state in the provision of services and goods. Outside the USA there were also economic pressures on television production industries resulting from the increased availability and importing of relatively cheap foreign television programs.

— *Political forces:* These included the impacts on broadcasting industries of shifts in geopolitical patterns resulting from changes such as the demise of communism and the redrawing of boundaries in Europe, as well as the political consequences of a global shift towards less state dominance in broadcasting industries.

— *Cultural forces:* These included the cultural effects associated with the increased availability of foreign - mostly USA - television program content.

— *Technological forces:* These were experienced mainly in the form of more access to new and more effective broadcasting technologies, e.g. satellite television, cable television and digital technologies. Theses forces were the result of dramatic world-wide advances in the development of information and communication technologies (ICTs) that is said to be creating a global information society.

Television industries world-wide have, as summarised in the following discussion that is based largely on the findings of Sinclair et al., tended to react differently to these forces.

Until the late 1970s only three regions in the world (North America, Latin America, and Australia) had mixed broadcasting systems, i.e. a combination of public and private sectors. Elsewhere state-owned broadcasting dominated in the form of either public service (Europe) or state-controlled (Asia and Middle East) transmissions. However, as the Fordist model of economic and political organisation began to lose support, there was a global shift from state regulation to market regulation. In many television industries this led to the introduction of privately owned commercial competitors to the public service monopolies - first in Italy, then in other European countries such as Germany, France, Holland and the United Kingdom.

The introduction of commercial television stations in turn led to an increase in channels and an increase in competition between these channels, accompanied by a new commercial force acting upon television industries in many countries: the market dominance of relatively cheap foreign television programming coming mainly from the USA. The reason for USA being able to provide this programming cheaply, lay in the USA audiovisual industry's competitive advantage of having unique access to the largest English speaking market in the world.

This represented an economic threat to local manufacturers of television programs, and in reaction political localisation measures appeared in some countries in the form of local television content quotas - both on a national level (e.g. in Canada) and on a regional level such as the European Union (EU). A related political reaction on a regional level was the EU's continued refusal to open their audiovisual industries to free trade under the GATT trade-in-services agreement, or to accept WTO authority in broadcasting matters.

Impact of TV Industries

The availability of relatively cheap foreign (mostly USA) television content led to contrasting reactions by different role-players in television industries world-wide. In most countries television audiences responded positively to the universal appeal of the new programs. Viewers were especially attracted to the their high technical standards, swift pace and action, familiarity of characters and predictability of outcome. This resulted in a world-wide consumer demand for new types of contents and formats. Broadcasters in these countries were generally happy to meet this need by broadcasting more and more imported programs. This resulted in a flow of cultural products from the USA to the rest of the world that was initially described as a one-way street.

The dynamics of this one-way flow of cultural products has been described in the work of cultural imperialism scholars such as Schiller: According to this view, such world patterns of communication flows mirror and reinforce system of economic and political domination. This perceived global cultural invasion contributed to defensive localisation actions on a national level by broadcasting decision makers, such as the censorship of foreign programs (e.g. in most Arab countries and in India), or the imposition of local program quotas on local broadcasters (e.g. in Canada). This protectionist type of reaction continues today in many countries.

The cultural imperialism discourse, the underlying rationale for such actions, has however come under increasing criticism on an empirical level and from theoretical paradigms such as postmodernism and theories of the active audience, as well as from the perspective that sees the mass media as a cultural system – where local cultures interact with the form and content of foreign media and so construct meaning around the media they consume.

Some countries - mostly those with well established and developed audiovisual industries - responded in technological terms to the increased access to new broadcasting technologies by adopting satellite television as a new broadcasting platform that could help them to reach out to new selected television audiences beyond national boundaries. Such a reaction can be described as localisation on a regional level, i.e. regionalism. Some of the countries outside of the USA who had responded to global technological forces by using satellite broadcasts to target new markets on a regional level, also reacted to the incoming cultural forces associated with foreign programming by producing more local television programs for the regional satellite broadcasts. Although most of these locally made programs tended to initially follow the general format of overseas programs, their content often later also featured unique local cultural elements. These programs were then broadcast both internally and across borders to specific types of audiences - usually audiences speaking the same language as the host country.

This process of increasingly broadcasting local programs containing unique cultural elements to geolinguistic regions has proved to be a formula for success. It has also resulted in a situation where world television flows can no longer always be described a one-way street of cultural influence emanating only from the USA, but rather as a patchwork quilt with many sources of regional influence.

Brazilian and Mexican satellite broadcasts to Latin American countries, Egyptian broadcasts to other Arab countries, and Indian broadcasts to diasporic audiences in other countries. Straubhaar calls this the regionalisation of television into multi-country markets linked by geography, language and culture – also known as geo-cultural markets. These developments can be seen as empirical evidence that calls into question the all-powerful medium conception of television and also the cultural imperialism theory. In stead they provide support for the active audience interpretation that states that audiences tend to use culturally foreign television content to suit their own needs, or for the viewpoint that television constitutes a cultural system in its own right, rather than a phenomenon in a context of culture.

As stated in the Broadcasting Green and White Papers, since the introduction of television in South Africa in 1976 until recently, the broadcasting system in this country was one of the most politicised broadcasting systems in the world. The South African Broadcasting Corporation (SABC) functioned as state broadcaster and had a near monopoly of the free-to-air (i.e. no decoder needed) broadcasting services in the country. The only competition for SABC television broadcasts was the pay channel M-Net that started broadcasting locally in 1986. During the 1990s the situation changed dramatically as local political forces accompanying the country's political transition to democracy, in conjunction with similar global political pressures, triggered the start of a local broadcasting reform process. This broadcasting reform process can be divided into three distinct but sometimes overlapping phases.

First, there was the broadcasting policy and legislative rethink that first preceded and then formed part of the multi-party political negotiations leading up to the fist democratic elections in 1994. The period since 1994 has been characterised by public inquiries into broadcasting structures taking place under the auspices of the Independent Broadcasting Authority (IBA). Finally, 1997 saw the start of a new Policy Process initiative by the Department of Communication that has linked future broadcasting changes to the process of telecommunications restructuring, and that has steadily eroded the power of the IBA.

The 1990s broadcasting policy debate was set in motion by the appointment of the Task Group on Broadcasting in South and Southern Africa in March 1990, and by media activists' responses to this Task Group. The ensuing debate reflected three views on how the future South African Broadcasting system should be structured: In agreement with the global shift from state regulation to market regulation, private broadcasters argued in favour of deregulation and commercialisation of broadcasting.

Civil society groups on the left advocated a public broadcaster operating in a pluralistic environment that is regulated by an independent agency, while political decision makers on the right preferred having only a state broadcaster, free from government interference. The two main protagonists—the African National Congress (ANC) and the then ruling National Party (NP) – generally followed different strategies in the debate. The ANC camp tended to participate by first articulating an "ideal" and then planning ways to achieve this, while the NP generally tended to look at what existed and at ways to re-order this.

Eventually the ANC decide to adopt the pluralist position. This view was then presented successfully to the multiparty Convention for a Democratic South Africa (CODESA) talks that started in September of 1991. The CODESA process finally led to the enactment of the Independent Broadcasting Authority (IBA) Act by the Transitional Executive Council in 1993.

The IBA Act stated that the radio and television markets should be opened to free-to-air commercial competition; it also provided for decentralised community broadcasting and for the state broadcaster to be transformed into a public broadcaster. To this end the SABC itself started developing a new Vision and Values framework, which in 1996 was to culminated in a re-launch of a new-look SABC aimed at protecting local culture and reflecting reality from a unique local perspective.

To what extent could the proposed changes to the South African broadcasting system, as formulated in the IBA Act, be seen as reactions to globalisation forces? In terms of Braman's typology of localisation processes, the changes can be described as the start of a move away from a primary mode of localisation response (supportive of existing traditional structures) to a secondary mode of localisation response (more reflective of a modernistic environment).

The decisions to end the monopoly of the state broadcaster, to introduce privately owned commercial competitors to the public service monopoly, and to reduce the influence of the state on the media, mirrored to a large extent the secondary localisation steps that had been taken internationally in many types of industries as reactions to a specific economic and political global force, namely the global disintegration of the Fordist model of economic and political organisation. On the other hand the IBA Act, being a product of the political compromises of the negotiations that ended apartheid, still entrenched the rights of existing broadcasters and therefore did not advocate a complete and radical restructuring of the broadcasting industry.

Transforming Broadcasting Reform Process

The first significant step in the broadcasting reform process after the 1994 elections was the creation of the Independent Broadcasting Authority to oversee future transformation of broadcasting. Next, in 1994, this new independent regulatory body launched its Triple Inquiry, a consultative investigation that dealt with the matter of whether or not to impose local content quotas for South African television and radio, the protection of public broadcasting services, and cross media control of broadcasting services. Throughout the inquiry the issue of local content quotas was the subject of considerable debate and criticism. On the one hand broadcasters opposed quotas as being an undemocratic economic burden imposed on them, while the record industry and television production industries (the intended beneficiaries of the system) were in favour of such quotas.

This imposition of local television content quotas that was being considered could, because of the emphasis on the local as a cultural reference point within a modernistic environment, be described as a secondary localisation measure taken in response to two types of globalisation forces impacting on television industries all over the world—a global cultural force and a global economic force.

The cultural force involved was, according to the reasoning of cultural imperialist scholars, the expectation that a high percentage of foreign television programming in local broadcasts would lead to a loss of cultural identity among viewers. This cultural threat was especially relevant in the light of the high priority that decision makers in the African National Congress (ANC) had been giving since 1994 to the promotion of nation-building via the media, e.g. by means of symbolic representations of national unification and reconciliation.

The global economic force was the market dominance of relatively cheap foreign television programming. For local broadcasters such as the SABC it was up to twenty five times more expensive to acquire a local television program for broadcasting than it was to import a program from the USA. This is not because South African local production costs of television programs are unduly high. In fact, local productions costs generally have been less than those of overseas production costs. The main reason for the difference in price is that the production costs of USA programs on offer to the international market have usually already been recovered in the USA, and consequently these programs can be exported at very cheap prices and still show a profit.

The IBA was therefore presented with a dilemma on how to react to globalisation forces. Should it react to the demands of global economic forces by allowing domestic television broadcasts to contain an unlimited amount of foreign programming content, thereby helping local broadcasters financially but damaging the local television production industry and possibly endangering the cultural identity of viewers? Alternatively, should the IBA rather react to the perceived cultural threat by applying measures restricting foreign content in local television broadcasts, thereby promoting local culture and hopefully also local content production, but adding to the financial burden of local broadcasters? In the end the IBA decided to act upon the cultural threat posed by foreign television programming, and proposed that a detailed set of local content quotas should be imposed on broadcasters. What qualified as "local" was, for the purposes of the quotas, stipulated by means of an elaborate set definitions and provisions.

Two other major issues that were addressed by the Triple Inquiry were how much of the broadcasting market the SABC should be allowed to retain, and how the future SABC should be financed. In its submissions to the IBA the SABC argued that it should be the sole national public broadcaster, and that as it would be required to broadcast country-wide in all eleven official languages, it could not be scaled down to much. The SABC also asked to retain all of its existing commercial radio and television channels in order to subsidise the public broadcasts. However, most of the other submissions to the IBA wanted a smaller SABC so that there would be room for new commercial broadcasters. In addition an influential group of civil society organisations wanted, in stead of just one national public broadcaster, a number of provincial public broadcasters and community broadcasters, all broadcasting locally in the languages of their respective regions or audiences.

The initial IBA recommendations that were released in 1995 reflected a compromise between the different submissions. The SABC was proposed as the sole national public broadcaster, i.e. no provincial public broadcasters were envisaged. However, it was also recommended that the SABC should sell off one of its three television channels and eight of its commercial radio channels. An intense lobbying of Parliament by the SABC resulted in the Parliamentary Portfolio Committee on Communications amending some recommendations.

The Triple Inquiry Report was approved in 1996. The amended report included stipulations that the SABC could retain all three of its television stations, and that it should sell six commercial radio stations to the private sector. These amendments constituted a significant political rebuff for the IBA. It was also approved that there should be three levels of broadcasting, and that provision must be made for a new commercial television station. Eventually this turned out to be the Midi-TV channel called e.tv, which started broadcasts in October 1998.

The next step in the broadcasting reform process was implementing the measures set out in the Triple Inquiry Report. For the SABC, 1996 was the year of many changes, starting in February with a re-launch of its three television channels. Now called SABC1, SABC2 and SABC3, each channel now broadcast to the nation as a whole rather than to separate white or black target audiences. Within six months this had resulted in a new audience profile characterised by fewer Afrikaans speaking viewers and a greater percentage of less affluent viewers.

The financial implications for the SABC's advertising income were severely negative. The financial crisis that was brewing within the SABC, was heightened by additional issues such as the increased cost of local content programming and the sell-off of six of the SABC's most lucrative commercial radio stations to groups with significant "black empowerment" credentials. In order to survive the SABC was forced to adopt a more commercial approach and to rely more heavily on imported programs than before.

In the mean time, the South African television quota system had also not been functioning smoothly. In November 1997 the Department of Arts, Culture, Science & Technology (DACST) convened a conference to discuss broadcasting local content issues. Of particular concern were problems that were being experienced with the quota system. The IBA decision makers had hoped that the local content quotas would result in local television programs being screened more and becoming more popular than before. They had also hoped that the resulting larger audiences would then generate larger advertising income for broadcasters, which could then at least counter some of the higher costs for broadcasters of having to buy more local rather than foreign programs. However, this had not happened.

Many local programs were indeed very popular and were enjoying larger audiences than most overseas programs, but this had not resulted in the hoped-for larger advertising income. It transpired that advertisers preferred to advertise in imported programs rather than in local programs, even when local programs' audiences were larger. On SABC3 in 1997 a single spot in the imported program Seinfeld cost R36000, but in the local program Muvhano it cost only a fraction of that, even though the latter program had almost twice the audience of the former.

Advertisers were simply spending less on African language broadcasts which were apparently not seen as significant markets. The SABC was already struggling to meet its local content quotas, and the unequal advertising income from local and overseas programs was aggravating the situation. After one year of broadcasting, the new commercial channel e.tv was also experiencing financial problems, and in October 1999 officially requested the IBA to lighten the channel's local content broadcasting burden.

In 1997 and 1998 the Department of Communication produced three documents - the Broadcasting Green Paper, the White Paper on Broadcasting Policy, and the Broadcast Bill— as part of a new Policy Process initiative that was aimed at providing a new framework for organising and regulating the South African broadcasting system. The Policy Process initiative reflected several changes in government priorities when dealing with the broadcasting industry. First, the new initiative brought with it a greater responsiveness to global technological forces, especially the convergence between telecommunications, information and broadcasting technologies. This led to measures aimed at merging aspects of the telecommunications and broadcasting industries, e.g. the two regulatory bodies. In turn this has meant that since 1997 broadcasting policy decisions have increasingly been affected by a telecommunications restructuring process that has been conducted in a less consultative and more state-controlled fashion than the broadcasting reform process. Broadcasting policy has also increasingly been seen by the government as part of a broader industrial and economic policy emphasising international competitiveness rather than cultural interests such as promoting national unity or identity.

By 1997 it was clear that the television industry was experiencing problems with regard to finding a way to make substantial use of foreign television programs without impacting negatively on issues such as the advertising revenue of local programs, the cultural identity of viewers, and the viability of the local television content production industry. As a result, the 1998 White Paper on Broadcasting Policy stipulated that the IBA must draw up a new plan for local content carriage by broadcasters, and that a new body, to be called the South African Broadcast Production Agency, must be formed to support and promote local content production.

The period between 1997 and 1999 was a difficult one for the IBA, for it was characterised by such severe tensions between the IBA and other role players in the broadcasting sector, that eventually the IBA's legitimacy was being called into question. Apart from frustrations arising among broadcasters because of lengthy procedures for applications and hearings and because of problems experienced with the IBA's local content quotas, the IBA was subjected to criticism on various fronts: This included criticism of the IBA's handling of the granting of the licence for the new commercial television station in 1997, and criticism of the IBA's handling of a 1997 dispute between the SABC and M-Net. The SABC was particularly frustrated by the IBA's inability to change M-Net's licensing conditions relating to the daily "open time" broadcasting slot, the operating of a second M-Net channel without a proper license, and M-Net's broadcasting of major sporting events in encoded form. To make matters worse for the IBA, allegations of financial mismanagement and of dissent within the IBA surfaced in the press and seriously harmed the body's public image.

Another major problem for the IBA in this period was the rift that was developing between it and Minister Naidoo. The Policy Process was also increasingly resulting in a loss of influence for the IBA, and in a transfer of power to the Minister and to the South African Telecommunications Regulatory Authority (SATRA). In January 1999 this conflict was highlighted by President Mandela refusing to sign the Broadcast Bill introduced to the National Assembly on the grounds that it transferred too much power to the Minister. An unexpected twist in this tale was that after the June 1999 elections Mr Jay Naidoo was replaced as Minister by Dr Ivy Matsepe-Casaburri. As the new Minister is someone with a definite interest in broadcasting – she was the first woman and black chairperson of the SABC Board – it will be interesting to see if the new appointment leads to any changes in the future official policy towards broadcasting in general or the IBA in particular.

The emphasis that the Policy Process placed on global technological opportunities also focused the attention of broadcasters more on the possible advantages of television transmissions via satellite. This broadened the scope of the South African broadcasting debate to include the broadcasting interests of neighbouring countries.

Ever since 1995, when the pay channel M-Net expanded its activities to include digital satellite broadcasts covering the whole of Africa, satellite broadcasting in South Africa had been dominated by the DStv satellite service provided through the distribution network company Multi-

Choice. Multi-Choice had previously been part of M-Net, and one of the reasons cited for the split from M-Net was for it to function as an international commercial company that would not be subject to social obligations that the IBA might impose on broadcasters. The SABC had also entered the satellite market with its free analogue AstraSat broadcasts in 1996, but its efforts to attract a sizeable audience following, and to include pay channels as part of the AstraSat service, did not succeed. Eventually, towards the end of 1998, the AstraSat service was discontinued.

Television broadcasters in neighbouring countries, such as the Lesotho Television Service, the Swaziland Broadcasting Corporation and the Namibian Broadcasting Corporation, were also not able to compete with the DStv satellite service. This meant that these transmissions from South Africa were now a source of regional cultural influence such as described by Tracey's patchwork quilt model. Because these earlier DStv broadcasts to the outside world consisted almost exclusively of overseas-produced material, the satellite transmissions could be seen in neighbouring countries not only as a potentially negative economic globalisation force from South Africa, but also as an indirect form of "cultural imperialism". One neighbouring broadcaster, the Namibian Broadcasting Corporation, resolved this issue by becoming part of the DStv bouquet of channels that could be received in Namibia.

Although the DStv satellite service had been much more successful financially within South Africa than AstraSat, the DStv broadcasts to the outside world initially featured mainly American entertainment that did not typically reflect unique South African cultural features. These international broadcasts had therefore not become known, as was the case with the Brazilian broadcasts containing telenovelas, as carriers of locally produced programs with an appeal to both local and certain foreign audiences.

The DStv broadcasts did not have a local equivalent for the internationally popular telenovelas, which can be described as a Latin American blend of soap opera, costume drama and situation comedy that – unlike North American soaps—have a beginning, a middle and an end. Viewed as reactions to global technological forces, both the SABC's and M-Net's adoption of satellite technology as international broadcasting platforms had – up to 1998—clearly not been an unqualified success. However, in November 1998 the SABC and Multi-Choice decided to settle past differences, and announced that they were embarking on a joint initiative in which an increased amount of local programs would be broadcast via the DStv satellite service to audiences all over Africa. Since November 16, the three SABC channels (SABC1, SABC2 and SABC3) have regularly been broadcast as part of the DStv bouquet. Since then the digital satellite service has also been transmitting two additional SABC television channels called Africa 2 Africa, a 24 hour African entertainment channel, and SABC Africa, a 24 hour African news and information channel.

This new international co-operative venture between local commercial broadcasting rivals can be described as a "restructuring" response to globalisation. An obvious advantage of the venture was that the existing three SABC channels now had a much wider audience, and therefore a greater potential to generate income for the SABC and for the South African TV industry. Other recently introduced DStv channels beaming locally produced content to audiences in neighbouring states are Channel O Sound Television, Summit TV, and kykNET.

The one factor that makes this joint initiative unique and qualitatively different from previous broadcasts to neighbouring countries, is that for some of the new DStv channels, "local" content is defined as meaning "African" content, and not just "South African" content. For example, the Africa 2 Africa channel regularly features films made by African producers, and while these products usually cannot compete with imported American films in terms of technical quality, they have a local "African" appeal for African audiences.

Similarly, SABC Africa is geared at being a vehicle that enables Africans to provide news about Africa for Africans, while Channel O Sound Television presents a variety of shows that feature music of black or African origin. This is expected to attract a relatively high viewership even in neighbouring states, for it has been shown that people prefer programs that are culturally close or familiar to them. Because this joint satellite initiative reacts to globalisation on the basis of the "local" of some channels being a willed construct that is to be interpreted in a broader sense than merely the geographic borders of one country, the initiative is an example of a tertiary localisation action on a regional level. It is also an example of the regionalisation of television into a multi-country geo-cultural market. While the approach does not directly address the financial concerns of rival broadcasters in neighbouring countries, it does create a new demand and market for the products and services of musicians, journalists, TV producers and film-makers of the neighbouring countries. In so doing, it goes some way in alleviating the economic and "cultural imperialist" concerns often associated with cross-border transmissions. This initiative is therefore seen as holding considerable promise for the future viability of South Africa's local television production industry.

From the foregoing discussion it is evident that during the 1990s the television industry in South Africa has experienced a broadcasting transformation process that took place in three main phases. Although broadcasting policy changes taking place during each phase were largely determined by the demands of the country's on-going process of political transition, it is evident that the increased exposure to a variety of global forces impinging on television industries world-wide also had an important influence on South Africa policy makers. It was found that each of the three phases of the broadcasting transformation process was characterised by different types of responses by policy makers to different types of globalisation forces. For example, during the first phase, the broadcasting rethink that took place between 1990 and 1994, the global forces that policy makers were most concerned with were forces of a political and economic nature.

Their responses to these forces were decisions that the television industry should in future be "reformed" in such a way that it acknowledged the importance of being in step with global trends, but without this leading to a radical restructuring of the existing broadcasting arena. This then led to legal stipulations aimed at transforming the state broadcaster to a public broadcaster and at opening up this public broadcaster to commercial competition. This first phase of broadcasting transformation can be described—In terms of Braman's typology of localisation processes—as the start of a move away from a primary mode of localisation response supportive of existing traditional structures, to a secondary mode of localisation response reflective of a modernistic environment.

During the second phase, in which the IBA had to decide on the practicalities of how the proposed broadcasting changes should be implemented, policy makers were confronted with a choice between responding to the economic implications or to the cultural implications of having a high percentage of foreign television programs in domestic broadcasts. Eventually IBA policy makers opted to go on the defensive against the cultural threat that foreign programs were perceived to hold for viewers, and they institute local content television quotas on broadcasters. As this response emphasised the local as a cultural reference point within a modernistic environment, it be described as a secondary localisation measure. Unfortunately however, it can be concluded that this measure was not very successful and that it resulted in a number of problems. In most cases these problems have in some way impacted negatively on the production of local television content.

During the third phase of broadcasting transition, the Policy Process initiated by the Department of Communication, policy makers were most responsive to the implications of global technological forces. It has resulted in "restructuring" types of responses to these forces, e.g., the merging of the telecommunications and broadcasting regulatory bodies (SATRA and the IBA). In this process there has been a policy shift that places more emphasis on economic priorities and industrial competitiveness, at the expense of cultural priorities such as promoting national identity among viewers. Decision were made mainly from a postmodern perspective that was aimed at promoting an information society, and the process can – in terms of the typology of Braman—-therefore be classified as a tertiary localisation action.

If one takes into account the lessons learnt from the reactions to globalisation of other television industries world wide, it seems that television industries stand to benefit most if their policy makers attempt to respond pro-actively to opportunities offered by global technological forces such as satellite broadcasting. This is in agreement with the approach of the Policy Process, which could auger well for the future. It is further contended that for any country's television industry as a whole, the most successful responses to globalisation are broadcasting initiatives involving a relatively high proportion of local content in outward bound international television satellite transmissions. Up to 1998 this had not been the case with the South African satellite broadcasts.

A recent joint initiative by the SABC and Multi-Choice has however resulted in an increased amount of local programs being broadcast via the DStv satellite service to neighbouring countries and the rest of Africa. This means that South African broadcasts now have a larger audience, and therefore a greater potential to generate income for the South African TV industry. It is a good example of what Straubhaar calls the regionalisation of television into a multi-country geo-cultural market.

Paradoxically, such cross-border satellite transmissions have the disadvantage that they could be experienced in neighbouring countries as being a negative globalisation force, both economically and culturally. The new joint DStv initiative has tried to counter this by defining the "local" content of some of the new DStv channels broadly as "African" content, and not only as "South African". In effect this has created a new potential market for the products and services of musicians, journalists, TV producers and film-makers of the neighbouring African countries. It is therefore concluded that this type of initiative holds much promise for the future of the South African television industry.

Bibliography

Barendt, Eric, *Broadcasting law: A Study of Regulation in Europe and the United States*, Oxford University Press, 1993.

Bennett, W. Lance, *The governing crisis: media, money and marketing in American elections*, New York, St. Martin's Press, 1992.

Bonnah Koomson, Anthony K., *A Handbook on electoral coverage for media practitioners*, Accra: Friedrich Ebert Stiftung, Ghana Office, 1995.

Coliver, Sandra, Merloe, Patrick and Naughton, Ann, (eds.), *Press Law and Practice*, London, ARTICLE 19, International Centre Against Censorship, 1993.

Darbishire, Helen, "Media and the Electoral Process" in Media and democracy, Council of Europe, Strasbourg, 1998.

Fletcher, Frederick J., *Media, elections and democracy*, Toronto: Dundurn Press, 1991.

Fox G.H., "The Right to Political Participation in International Law," ,*Yale Journal of International Law* 539 1992.

Johnston, Carla B., *Election coverage: blueprint for broadcasters*, Focal Press, Stoneham, 1991.

Joslyn, Richard, *Mass media and elections, Reading, Mass.*, Addison-Wesley Pub. Co, 1984.

Lange, Yasha, *Media and elections: handbook*, Strasbourg, Council of Europe Publications, 1999.

Raymond Louw, *A Handbook on the Media and Electoral Law*, Electoral Institute of Southern Africa, Johannesburg, 1999.

Mancini, Paolo, and Swanson, L. (eds.), *Politics, Media and Modern Democracy,* Westport, CT: Praeger Publishers, 1996.

Mickiewicz, Ellen, and Firestone, Charles, Television and elections, Queenstowne, MD, The Aspen Institute, 1992.

Pragnell, Anthony, "Freedom and control: the elements of democratic broadcasting services", Dusseldorf, European Institute for the Media, 1990.

Yasha Lange and Andrew Palmer (eds), *Media and Elections: a Handbook, European Institute for the Media,* Dusseldorf, 1995.

Index